Inspiration™

FOR LGBT STUDENTS & THEIR ALLIES

ENCOURAGEMENT

HUMOR & MOTIVATION

FOR

LGBT STUDENTS

& THEIR ALLIES

BY

LGBT STUDENTS

& THEIR ALLIES

The Collegiate
EmPowerment Company, Inc.
www.Collegiate-EmPowerment.com
Toll Free: 1.877.338.8246

D0162257

The
Collegiate
EmPowerment
Company, Inc.

"Helping You Take Higher Education Deeper™"

Co Authored By: ANTHONY J. D'ANGELO,
STEPHEN D. COLLINGSWORTH JR., MIKE ESPOSITO,
GABRIEL HERMELIN, RONNI SANLO, LYDIA A. SAUSA
AND SHANE L. WINDMEYER

Published by:

The Collegiate EmPowerment Company, Inc.

"Helping You Take Higher Education Deeper™"

EASTON, PENNSYLVANIA 18040
WWW.COLLEGIATE-EMPOWERMENT.COM

Printed with Pride in The United States Of America
ISBN: 0-9646957-4-X

BOOKS ARE AVAILABLE IN QUANTITY DISCOUNTS WHEN USED FOR STUDENT DEVELOPMENT AND RECOGNITION. FOR PRICING INFORMATION PLEASE SEE THE LAST PAGE AT THE BACK OF THIS BOOK. THANK YOU.

We would like to thank all the contributing authors for permission to reprint their submissions. Please refer to the back of this book for individual acknowledgements.

The Inspiration Book Series

Here's What People Are Saying About
Inspiration for LGBT Students and Their Allies™

"Everyone, young or old, needs heroes and role models. This book is filled with them. But unlike many heroes and role models, these wonderful people are not inaccessible, or high on a pedestal. They are ordinary folks doing extraordinary things. Read their words -- and prepare to be inspired!"
Dan Woog, Author of Jocks: True Stories of America's Gay Male Athletes and Jocks 2: Coming Out To Play.

"WOW! Tears of recognition, identification, and understanding will definitely flow in many people who read these vignettes. Inspiration for LGBT students and allies comes at a time when ALL of us in the community need to remember the human side of who we are. These stories will truly inspire us. Buy extra copies of this book because you will want to keep one and give others away!"
Wendy Stubbs, MA, University of South Dakota, Co-Advisor to the USD Gay Lesbian Bisexual Alliance

"Wow, such powerful voices that need to be heard but more often go silent. This collection is wonderful not only for students but also for student affairs professionals who wish to get a glimpse into the lives of some of the students they serve. Of course it will be a great companion to students who are struggling with their own identity and for those allies who support them. Great job, thanks."
Judy Albin, National Association of Student Personnel Administrators (NASPA) Chair, GLBT Knowledge Community And Senior Associate Director, Penn State University

"No matter how many barriers we overcome, how many firsts we enjoy, how many opportunities we demand access to, we must never forget the fear and shame that many young people feel as they struggle with their sexual orientation. It's hard, and it's scary, and it's life shaping. We have a responsibility to demonstrate to them that a joyous, rewarding, achievement-filled life can be theirs. If this book boosts the self-esteem of one young gay man or woman, or if one friend chooses an embrace over awkwardness, then this book has served its purpose."
T.J. Sullivan, Managing Partner, CAMPUSPEAK, Inc.

"As a previous student leader myself, and in my present work with LGBT student leaders, I know our fight is one that is seldom appreciated. It is work that longs for this type of encouragement. Inspiration for LGBT Students & Their Allies is an uplifting book that will move any student to understand why our continuing battle for equality is an important one"
M Chad Wilson, Co-Founder, Campus PrideNet and Former Student Leader from Appalachian State University

What People Are Saying About This Book

"I wish a book like this had existed when I was a student in the late 60's....it could have given me the knowledge that I was not alone in my sexual identity struggle....and given me the strength to be out and proud and productive at a time when I was so confused and depressed. I would have loved to give it to my parents."
Mitchell Gold, Founder and President Mitchell Gold Company

"These stories will touch your heart and soul – and remind you of what it means to live with courage every single day."
**Elizabeth Randazzese, MSW, Co-Author of
Inspiration for Student Leaders & EmPower X! Coach**

"Succinctly written and engaging, these stories will be, without question, enormously supportive of LGBT students. Equally impressive will be the value of the stories to allies, who often want to be helpful, but are confused and fearful of saying the wrong thing."
**Pamela W. Freeman, Co-Author, Out on Fraternity Row and Secret Sisters
Associate Dean of Students, Indiana University**

"Who of us doesn't need to be uplifted and affirmed in dealing with something as insidious as homophobia? These stories will touch your heart and strengthen your resolve. They are funny, insightful, moving,thought-provoking, and, most importantly, heart-felt. You will carry their images into your days and they will make a difference in your life."
**Doug Bauder, Ordained Pastor for the Moravian Church and Coordinator of
Indiana University's GLBT Student Support Service Office**

"Since the beginning of humankind people have gained strength, hope and power from joining together to share their personal stories. This book follows that work. As we spend time with this book, our isolation dissolves and we find ourselves joining with others in this great circle of love and support."
**Gregg Cassin, Inspirational Speaker, Gay Dad, Co-Chair of AIDS,
Medicine & Miracles**

I think this book is an invaluable resource that should be on every campus and used in cultural diversity courses and trainings. The stories are moving and empowering. They provide a source of information for those outside the LGBT community and a source of strength and support for those within the LGBT community.
**Kylar Broadus, State Legislative Manager and Counsel for the Human Rights
Campaign and Assistant Professor at Lincoln University**

This Book is
Dedicated to You,
For Having the
Courage to
Be Who
You Are

Table of Contents

Support The People Who Support LGBT Students

In the spirit of Taking Higher Education Deeper,
The Collegiate EmPowerment Company, Inc.,
recognizes The National Consortium of Directors of LGBT
Resources In Higher Education as the Charitable Benefactor
of Inspiration for LGBT Students & Thier Allies ™.

The Collegiate EmPowerment Company will donate One Dollar from every book sold to The Consortium. This money will help support The Consortium as it pursues its Vision & Mission.

The combined vision and mission of the National Consortium of Directors of Lesbian Gay Bisexual and Transgender (LGBT) Resources in Higher Education (The Consortium) is to achieve higher education environments in which LGBT students, faculty, staff, administrators, and alumni have equity in every respect.

The goals of the Consortium are:
- To support colleagues and develop curriculum to professionally enhance this work
- To consult with higher education administrators in the interest of improving campus climate and services for LGBT faculty, staff, students, administrators, and alumni/ae
- To advocate for institutional policy changes and program development that recognize the needs of LGBT people

NATIONAL
CONSORTIUM
OF DIRECTORS
▼
OF LGBT RESOURCES IN HIGHER EDUCATION

For more information please visit www.lgbtcampus.org

The Inspiration Book Series

Welcome To The Inspiration Book Series!

Dear Reader,

Thank you for reading Inspiration for LGBT Students & Their Allies. The book you are holding has been made possible by people just like you. This book, as well as the entire Inspiration Book Series, is a compilation of stories of encouragement, empowerment and motivation by college students for college students. Simply put, this book is for YOU and by YOU.

This whole "Inspiration Revolution" was started by myself and two college students, Amy Connolly-Weber and Dan Oltersdorf the co-authors of Inspiration for Resident Assistants. The vision which we had back in 1999 has now manifested itself into a seven part book series. This book is number four in the series and we've got three more on the way!

It has been said that "Every new beginning comes from some other beginning's end." And this is exactly what has lead to the creation of Inspiration For LGBT Students & Their Allies. The seeds for this book were planted in December of 2001 at the Association For Fraternity Advisors (AFA) Annual Conference. I was attending the conference in conjunction with the national release of Inspiration For Greeks. This launch marked "the end" of over six months of labor & love. Yet little did I know, this ending created a new beginning, thanks in part to one person, Shane Windmeyer.

Shane was also attending the AFA Conference. Although I had never met Shane before, I was quite familiar with his ground- breaking work regarding LGBT & Greek Life Issues. Shane approached our book distribution table and ask one of our team members, "Have you guys ever considered doing an Inspiration Book for LGBT students?" This was the one question that needed to be asked and it was Shane who had the courage to ask it.

At the same time we were launching Inspiration for Greeks, we were also coming to the completion of Inspiration for Student Leaders, which was slated for release in February of 2002. We were planning to focus our on energies on Inspiration For Student Athletes as our next book in the series. But thanks to Shane our plans changed. As John Lennon said, "Life is what happens to you when you are making plans for the future." I told Shane that I was considering developing an Inspiration Book for the LGBT Community, but I needed to develop a solid co-author team. He told me he could help and that is exactly what he did. Within 45 days we had an incredible co-author team on board and our call for submissions had made it's way through every list serve. And that's when things really began to take off...

Never before have we experienced such a flood of submissions for an Inspiration Book. During the month of March 2002 alone, we were receiving an average of 10 submissions a day! In total we received over 500 submissions for consideration for members of the LGBT community from across the globe!

I would find myself reading submission after submission late into the night. I was humbled, inspired and often moved to tears, as I began to fully grasp the passion, courage and determination of the LGBT Community. As Emerson once proclaimed, "Who you are shouts so loudly, I need not hear a word you say." My friends, in the following pages of this book, you have spoken. And I have no doubt that the world will here you.

I've have always been an ally to the LGBT Community, but as a result of this project I am proud to call myself an Advocate of the community. It is truly an honor and a privilege to be associated with a book of this quality and character. It is a representation of who we are and all that we can become, together. For none of us in this world are alone.

May you be proud of who you are!

Anthony J. D'Angelo,

The Creator Of The Inspiration Book Series™

About The Authors:

Anthony J. D'Angelo is the Founder of The Collegiate EmPowerment Company (CEC) and The Creator of *The Inspiration Book Series*™. In 1995 at the age of 23, Mr. D'Angelo made a decision to commit his life to Take Higher Education Deeper™. Since making this commitment, he and his team have empowered over 1 million college students from over 1,000 college campuses throughout North America. He is the co-author of 6 books including the #1 NY Times Bestseller, *Chicken Soup for The College Soul*®. Anthony has been hailed by CNN as "The personal development guru of his generation" and has been featured in several national media outlets including CNN, SPIN Magazine and Oprah Magazine. He and his loving wife, Christine, make their home in the Lehigh Valley Area of Pennsylvania, where they enjoy nature, kayaking and frequent trips to the Jersey Shore.

Stephen D. Collingsworth Jr. has been involved with the queer political movement since 1987. He is currently the Assistant Director of the Multicultural Center and Coordinator for Queer Issues at Williams College in Massachusetts. He serves on the boards of the Berkshire Stonewall Community Coalition, the Western Massachusetts LGBTQ Youth Coalition and the LGBT Political Alliance of Western Massachusetts. He received his BA and MA from The Ohio State University and serves on the Advocacy Committee for the OSU GLBT Alumni Society. In addition to being the first Queer Issues Coordinator at Williams, he served as the first Education Coordinator for Stonewall Columbus,

Columbus' LGBT Center, as well as the first Director of the Kaleidoscope Youth Coalition, Columbus' LGBT Youth Center. He and his partner Don reside in the beautiful Berkshire Mountains on the borders of Vermont and New York with their two cats and a huge, goofy mutt named Bombadil.

Mike Esposito earned a Bachelor of Arts degree in journalism at Morehead State University in Kentucky. At Morehead, through work in student government and Sigma Nu fraternity, he developed an interest in the student affairs profession. In graduate school at Western Kentucky University, Mike came out as a gay man. After achieving a Masters of Arts in Education degree, he accepted the Greek Life and Involvement Coordinator position at The University of Montana—Missoula. He was a founding member of the Western Montana Gay and Lesbian Community Center, served on the PRIDE! board of directors and was a writer for OutSpoken lgbt Magazine. Currently, Mike is the Student Organization Coordinator at Boise State University, in Idaho. His activism continues through work on The Community Center board of directors and through his regular column ("Singular Wit") in Diversity lgbt Newsmagazine.

Gabriel Hermelin has been a loud member of the Queer community for 16 years as a public speaker, diversity trainer, workshop facilitator and activist. As a college student Gabriel was involved in campus activism as the President of the Auraria Queer Alliance, the VP of Communication in the Student Government Assembly and as the Speaker's Bureau and Safe Zone Project Coordinator in the Office of GLBT Student Services. Gabriel has a BA in

Interpersonal Communication Theory from Metropolitan State College of Denver in Denver, CO and an MS in Conflict Analysis and Resolution with a specialization in College Student Personnel Administration from Nova Southeastern University in Fort Lauderdale, FL. Currently Gabriel is attending seminary at Pacific School of Religion in Berkeley, CA. You may learn more about Gabriel at www.gabrielhermelin.com

 **Ronni Sanlo** is a pioneer in the LGBT community who currently serves as the director of the UCLA Lesbian Gay Bisexual Transgender (LGBT) Campus Resource Center and a lecturer in the UCLA Graduate School of Education. Dr. Sanlo earned her bachelor's degree from the University of Florida, and a masters and doctorate in education from the University of North Florida in Jacksonville, Florida. Her research area is sexual orientation issues in education and higher education. Before joining the staff at UCLA, Ronni was the LGBT Center director at the University of Michigan.

Ronni is the founding chair of the National Consortium of LGBT Campus Resource Center Directors and currently, she serves on the national board of the Council for the Advancement of Standards in Higher Education (CAS). As a prolific writer, Ronni is the author of three books; *Working with LGBT College Students: A Handbook for Faculty and Administrators*; *Unheard Voices: The Effects of Silence on Lesbian and Gay Educators*; and *Our Place on Campus: LGBT Programs and Services in Higher Education* (Greenwood Press) and serves on the editorial board of the *Journal of Gay and Lesbian Issues in Education*. Dr. Ronni Sanlo is a frequent speaker, consultant, author, and presenter on LGBT issues in higher education and is the originator of

the award-winning Lavender Graduation, an event that cele-
brates the lives and achievements of LGBT students. Most of all
Ronni is the proud grandmother of two little girls and the
daughter of outrageous PFLAG parents.

Lydia A. Sausa is currently an Adjunct Professor at San

Francisco State University, in the Human
Sexuality Studies Program. Lydia received a M.S.
Ed. in Human Sexuality Education and is a
Ph.D. candidate at the University of
Pennsylvania. Lydia has been working for more
than seven years as a Professional Consultant,
Trainer, and Sexuality Educator providing dynamic and innova-
tive in-service trainings and educational workshops assisting
schools and health care organizations improve their outreach,
education, and services to lesbian, gay, bisexual, and trans youth.
Lydia has also published journal articles specifically on the educational and health care needs of trans youth and has presented
at numerous regional, national, and international conferences.
For more information or to schedule a workshop presentation
or staff training for your school or organization, please contact
www.lydiasausa.com.

Shane L. Windmeyer is one of the foremost
educators on sexual orientation issues on college
campuses today. Windmeyer is the co-editor of
two ground-breaking books, *Out on Fraternity
Row: Personal Accounts of Being Gay in a College
Fraternity* and *Secret Sisters: Stories of Being
Lesbian and Bisexual in a College Sorority*. He joined Phi Delta
Theta Fraternity in the Spring of 1992 while attending Emporia
State University. He recalls coming out to his fraternity brothers
as "one of his most rewarding undergraduate experiences" and

the purpose for his work. As a result, he founded and serves as coordinator of the Lambda 10 Project National Clearinghouse for Gay, Lesbian, Bisexual Greek Issues to help support gay, lesbian, bisexual members of the college fraternity and to educate on issues of homophobia within the college Greek system. In 2002, Windmeyer launched Campus Pride.Net, a new online national network for gay, lesbian, bisexual, transgender, queer college student leaders and their allies.

Windmeyer has been a professional guest speaker on over 120 college campuses since the release of his first book and has presented at numerous educational conferences dealing with Greek life and, or gay, lesbian, bisexual issues on a local, regional and inter/national levels. Windmeyer has been featured on IN THE LIFE TV for their Fall Season Premiere episode aired on PBS and his work has been the focus of national attention from the New York Times and other national press. Windmeyer graduated from Emporia State University with a bachelor's degree in Communication and received his master's degree in Higher Education and Student Affairs Administration from Indiana University.

Acknowledgements and Appreciation

This Project would not be possible without the support, guidance and inspiration of the following individuals. We are very, very grateful for you.

Anthony would like to say thank you to:
My loving wife Christine. You stand here with me despite the storms. You are simply an amazing soul. I cherish you dear friend. To my family. Not one, but two. I am blessed to have your continuos love and support. Your faith in me will never be forgotten. To Elizabeth Randazzese & Dr. Jarrod Spencer, my associates and inspiring friends. Taralynn Ross, of Browndog Design. Thank you once again for bringing life to our Vision. To Dr. Raymond Friday for your generosity & wisdom. To Dwayne Stevens, keeping things at the CEC sane. To Dan Sullivan & The Strategic Coach Team, thank you transforming a young rugged individualist into a team thinker. The world will be forever transformed thanks to what you guys do! Here's to our life long relationship. And most of all, to the Clients, Customers & Students of The Collegiate EmPowerment Company: Our firm is a reflection of all we have learned from you. You are our greatest gift. Thank you for allowing us to Help You Take Higher Education Deeper. It is an honor to serve you. Here's to our continued partnership & success!

The Members of The Coauthor Team Would Like To Thank:

Stephen would like to acknowledge his parents, grandmother, and Donny without whose strength he would not have found the ability to be himself.

Mike thanks: My Mom, the best support any queer could hope for. Dale, for making my coming out so easy. I love you both.

Gabriel would like to say: Thank you to my father for being such an inspiration, and supporting me through my many twists and turns in life.

Ronni is grateful for her courageous and precious UCLA students who remind her every day why she does this work, and to Peggy Corgi who gives good bark.

Lydia would like to thank everyone for their wonderful submissions, especially those from queer youth and trans individuals who have courageously and generously shared their stories of inspiration, education, and advocacy for change.

Shane would like to say: I love you, Tom. Thanks Mom, Dad, Sis for your love always. Shout "out" to the students who dare to stand up for others, no matter who they are!

Most of all we want to thank the hundreds of people who send us submissions for this project. You proved to us what we thought all along; This is a book whose time has come. Without you this book would not be. Thank you!

A Proud History
by Stephen D. Collingsworth

Many people ask me, "Why Queer Pride? We don't need Straight Pride!" My answer is usually a quick, flip "Well… maybe straight people haven't anything to be proud of!" Of course, that's not the case. The difference is that heterosexuals do not need to express their pride. There has not been a time when heterosexuals, as a group, were forced into silence in society. The truth is, they take themselves for granted. There is always an assumption of heterosexuality. Generally speaking, society does not take into consideration that people may be other than heterosexual.

But, to answer the question, "Why do we need Queer Pride?," quite simply, because our young people are killing themselves every day. According to the U.S. Department of Health and Human Services, one out of every three teenagers who commit suicide is gay, lesbian, or bisexual. It's suspected to be even higher in the transgendered community. We need Queer Pride so every one of these beautiful young people know they are not alone: that they are okay. Even though one in four gay, lesbian and bisexual teenagers are kicked out of their homes (once again, it's suspected to be even higher for transgendered youth), we need to let them know that it is not they, it is their parents who are at fault.

We need Queer Pride because until we end the silence and destroy the closet we will always be second class citizens. In 38 states we can be fired because of our sexual orientation. Our children are often taken from us because of our sexual orientation. In Florida a judge granted custody of a child to his father who was convicted and served his time for second degree murder rather than give custody to the mother who was a lesbian and who was forbidden to see the child in the presence of her partner. We won't even get into Sodomy Laws. We need Queer Pride to reaffirm who we are and to glean the strength to hold our heads high in the face of adversity.

We also have a right to be very proud of our people! After all, queer people have been some of the movers and shakers of society. We have created beauty and uplifted souls.

We are theologians: The Pharaoh Akhenaten introduced monotheism to the world. The monk Desiderius Erasmus was one of the greatest thinkers of the Reformation. St. Augustine, in his book Confessions, writes "I felt his soul and mine were one soul in two bodies." Then there are the popes: Leo X, John XXII, Julius II, Paul II, Sixtus IV, Alexander VI, Julius III, and Benedict IX (some good, some bad). King James I of England commissioned the best known version of the Bible and was known far and wide by his people as "Queen James."

We are generals: Alexander the Great conquered the Western world. Julius Caesar tried to follow suit. Richard the Lionhearted preferred the Crusades to ruling England. Frederick the Great wasn't known as "Great" for nothing.

We are great artists: Michelangelo painted the ceiling of the Sistine Chapel. Leonardo DaVinci painted a smile that has left billions of people wondering, and served a prison sentence for a sodomy charge. Thanks to Andy Warhol, we will never look at a soup can the same way again.

We are educators: Plato, Socrates, Sappho, George Washington Carver.

We are Human Rights Activists: Sojourner Truth, Eleanor Roosevelt, Barbara Jordan, Susan B. Anthony, Bayard Rustin.

We are writers: Langston Hughes, Emily Dickinson, Shakespeare, Willa Cather, James Baldwin.

We are entertainers: Josephine Baker, Gladys Bentley, Bessie Smith, Ma Rainey.

We enlighten. We uphold truth. We spread beauty.

Our history is rich with great figures who have molded and shaped society. As with everyone, their personal life, loves, trials and tribulations, shaped who they were. Is it important that we know whom they went to bed with? No, not really. Is important that we know they were gay, lesbian, bisexual, transgendered or queer? Definitely. Their sexuality helped mold them, shape them. It allowed them to see the world in a different way. To see what things might be, and not get mired in what things are: to think beyond the box.

We have Queer Pride because we cannot be silent any longer. Those fabulous Drag Queens and Butch Dykes in the Stonewall Riots of 1969 showed us the power of speaking out and acting out. Of being proud of who we are: of not hiding. We refuse any longer to isolate any part of ourselves. The great writer and activist Audre Lorde said "There will always be someone begging you to isolate one piece of yourself, one segment of your identity above the others, and say, 'Here, this is who I am.' Resist that trivialization. I am not JUST a lesbian. I am not JUST a poet. I am not JUST a mother. Honor the complexity of your vision and yourselves." Sister Audre, every day when we speak and say "Yes I Am," we celebrate all aspects of our being. In being brave enough to do so, we also dare to share ourselves with the world. ▼

*This submission is also available in poster format.
To purchase a poster please contact: The Collegiate EmPowerment Company
by calling toll free: 1-877-338-8246 or email: PosterInfo@Collegiate-EmPowerment.com.
Posters also be viewed and purchased online at: www.Collegiate-EmPowerment.com.
Thank you for your interest!

Onion As A Metaphor
by Patricia Kevena Fili

Be not confused
The shell you'll see
Is just that
A covering
Of pure essence.
When peeled away,
Witness a conscience,
Intuition,
A truth unfettered
By masks unwanted.
When peeled away,
Experience something truly unique:
A free human spirit,
Unrestricted by conventions
And norms
In a world
Frightened
By beauty and spirit. ▼

A Guy Who Happened to Be Gay
by Anthony J. D'Angelo

I became an ally to the LGBT community because I knew a guy who "happened to be gay". It was during my first year in college at West Chester University in Pennsylvania. I came to college as an eighteen year old white heterosexual male from a small provincial town in south central Pennsylvania. I was straighter than straight.

Fortunately I was raised in a family of unconditional love and support. We were always taught to be accepting of others differences regardless or race, religion or status. Yet one thing we did not have was a sensitivity to the LGBT community. After all the small town of New Cumberland, PA is not the cosmopolitan epicenter of the universe. Oh, we were exposed to alternative lifestyles. Like the "dyke" bar on Third Street and to the "fags" on City Island, and those "weirdo" cross dressers that we would see in downtown Harrisburg, but as you can see, these references where not exactly positive. It wasn't until my first year in college that my perceptions began to change.

My first few weeks at college were challenging. I missed my friends. I wanted to go home. Things began to get better for me as I went out and got involved on campus. I really found my place at West Chester by getting involved in the student government association (SGA). As the fall semester progressed I became more and more involved with SGA. There I had the chance to met some incredible fellow student leaders. The great thing about being in SGA when you are a first year student is most of the members are older. You get to become friends with the people who you look up to. I remember them all, yet there was one guy who I really looked up to. His name was Ted.

Ted was a good looking 22 year old senior majoring in communications, whose dress and appearance were always immaculate. Although I was not as close with Ted as I was with other members, he was a person who I deeply respected. Being very articulate and well spoken, when Ted spoke people listened. If an important issue was being debated on the senate floor, members would often wait to cast their vote until Ted had the opportunity to voice his opinion. Often times people would side with Ted not only because of his leadership and charisma, but because what he was said simply made sense.

In my mind what made Ted most unique was that he was not a regular senate member, in that he did not represent a specific school or college such as Business, Music or Education. Nor was he a representative of a specific class such as the senior class. No, what made Ted unique to me was that he represented the GSU, The Gay Student Union. I can recall how "nice" I thought it was that he was willing to represent "those gay people" at student government meetings. Needless to say it never dawned on me that he might just be one of "those gay people"! Not until the end of the fall semester.

It was during a heated debate over whether or not we should continue to support ROTC on West Chester's campus. Several students spoke on the matter. Many in favor of the program and an equal number of opposed to it. The discussion was passionate and went on for over an hour. Tempers were flaring. My blood began to boil as I was getting ready to take my stand in favor of the ROTC Program. I thought to myself, "I can't believe these damn communists want to get rid of ROTC! That's un-American!" (Keep in mind at the time I was an 18 year gung-ho American kid who listened to Metallica and sported a high & tight marine haircut. West Chester was actually my fourth choice for college. My top three schools were The United States Merchant Marine Academy, The Citadel and The Virginia Military Institute. West Chester was my safety school. It ultimately saved me in more ways than one.) Yet for some reason, I, like many of the other SGA members who had yet to voice their opinion, sat there waiting. We were waiting to hear what Ted had to say.

As Ted took the floor the energy of the room began to change. An almost serene calmness overtook the senate chamber. Not because of what Ted was about to say, but because what we were about to hear. Ted began to speak.

"As a student here at West Chester University I find it unacceptable for us as a student body to support the ROTC Program. The fact of the matter is that the Untied States Military & the ROTC program discriminates against homosexuals. This means that openly gay students on our very own campus would be denied access to this program. I simply cannot support it, because I am an openly gay man myself."

When I heard Ted say this, time began to slow down. I began an internal dialogue with myself. Here one of "those people" were right in front of me. Live in the flesh. This guy never hit on me or tried to convert me, like my preconceived stereotypes had led me to believe. I remember thinking to myself, I respected this person before I knew he was gay, so why would I not respect him now?

And that is when my life changed. For me this was a cathartic moment; a moment in my life I will never forget. A moment which forced me to question all my beliefs about what it means to be gay, what it means to be straight and most of all what it means to be human. For me it was an epiphany.

This guy simply lived his life. This guy was who he was, not what he was. This guy was a fellow student of mine. This guy was in SGA with me. This guy was someone who I admired and deeply respected. This guy was someone who had the courage to be himself. This guy was someone who lived his life with dignity and grace. This guy was someone who taught me to think differently. This guy was a guy who happened to be gay. ▼

My Last Razor
by Jordan

In society we have unwritten rules
That everyone follows and no one duels:
Girls will shave their legs and some guys will shave their faces
And if one so chooses, they will shave other places.
Choosing not to stick to the pic,
I threw away my Bic
Disposable razor away. It is now waiting
In the trash while girls are hesitating
As to whether they are prickly enough
To shave. I don't huff and puff
Worrying about making my legs silky smooth
So I impress that rude, homophobic dude
That whispered, "Dyke!" today as I made
My way down the hall. That was my last shaving blade,
That I threw away with my feelings mixed.
But that meant no more shaving cream and nicks,
Razor burn or lotion.
And what a commotion
It stirs when my legs are in view
Of my mom, she says, "If you
Are going in public with me then I don't
Want to see your hairy legs." "Then I wont
Go with you today." I say with a sad heart.
She looks the other way and starts
Asking, "Why can't you be like all of the

Other girls I see?" "Because mom, that isn't me
Or who I need to be to be happy." Why
Is it that when a girl or guy
Drifts from the norm
They are pelted and thorned
With criticism from people
They don't know? It is feeble
To discriminate
I associate
With the feelings and pride
Of the oppressed, I'm on their side
Of the fight. All night and day
I strive to be the way
I feel inside. I wont and can't
Hide who I am with the leg of a pant. ▼

The Parable of the Eventual Suicide
by Sean C. Hayes

When I begin to worry about my future and my ability to find a fulfilling, adequately paying job – I need only look at advertisements in gay magazines to find some consolation. To think, that while people struggle to obtain degrees in business or medicine, all it takes to sell anything to gay men is a photograph of a well-built shirtless guy who, presumably, uses the product being sold – whether it's beer, a prescription drug, a book or an electric tooth brush – snap a picture of some hunky guy and the story writes itself.

The only possible career hazard would surmount itself, if tragically, the world were to face a shortage of men whose bodies are deemed well enough to sell products. When I hit Bourbon Street in New Orleans last fall, I realized however that was little danger of a shirtless man shortage. In late October, a Thursday night, at 6 p.m., the gay end of the street was 75 hairless, shirtless men deep on every side. Evidently, they all still subscribed to Madonna's '80s "underwear as outerwear" trend as well. If, suddenly that chunk of Bourbon Street were to float off into the Mississippi, between the 500 shirtless wonders, there would not be enough fabric to knit a sail.

The title of the John Cheever novel, "Oh What a Paradise it Seems" occurred to me, but was tapered by a comment made by a man standing near me. "All these guys care about is youth and looking good, because they all figure they'll be dead by 30." It seemed to make sense as not anywhere did I see anyone aged, anyone overweight or anybody whose company would be anything more than directions to the after-party. It occurred to me that at 23, I was pathologically afraid to age. I once read about an actress, Pier Angeli, who though still beautiful offed herself at 39 because she couldn't bear the notion of turning 40. It occurred to me, that for years, me and many people I know were essentially committing eventual suicide – going through the motions of preparing for the future, while all the while each day seemed to bring us closer to a kind of gay death, an extinction of youth and beauty that in this niche culture marks an utter loss of vitality.

In this rush to an extreme ideal of beauty, success and acting generally fabulous, the loss occurs not only of the spiritual and emotional side of life, but of wisdom and culture. In essence, young gay men are a culture that is drifting off into an oblivion of uncertainty. To say, as W.B. Yeats, that the "center does not hold" would be to lose sight of the fact that the center is not present, only surface – a veneer as flimsy as one those ads in a magazine.

I have always rolled my eyes at critiques of the fashion industry, advertisers and celebrities, as though "regular people" don't have the capacity to distinguish fantasy and reality. But these seem to be the only images open to gay men. Almost every young gay man I knows wants to be a model, claims to have worked as a model or dated one. I know precious few however whose ambition it is to make a difference in the world, help people find peace or justice or make a contribution even to the gay community.

The freedom for the eventual suicide and the loss of the fear of aging in people at the prime of their lives must begin with a reexamination of what we truly find to be beautiful and meaningful. Oscar Wilde said that art was the combination of surface and symbol, not merely a political statement but also not merely a pretty object. He said it was 'perilous' to read too deeply into the symbolism, but not to thoroughly ignore it either. I suggest that no one hide themselves in a monastery or become a hermit – or fail to look at sexy men on principle – I just wonder if a beauty obsession should work within other priorities, and not become a be-all end-all obsession.

To quote another poem by Yeats, "An aged man is but a paltry thing,/A tattered coat upon a stick, unless/Soul clap its hands and sing, and louder sing/for every tatter in its mortal dress…"

I once thought I too would go out in a veritable hail of bullets like the glamorous burnouts of old Hollywood, too tragic to survive in a cruel world, but who knows, maybe when beauty fades, another kind of beauty awaits. ▼

Closet Door
by Heather Hershey

So I am a lesbian.
Yeah that's right!
Never saw it coming,
Did you?
Surprised?
Shocked?
Horrified?
All three? Maybe...
Don't worry,
I'm not.
It's okay,
For me anyway.
What about you?
How do you feel?
Scared?
Happy?
Confused?
Me, all three.
But it's all right,
I'm accepting of it.
It was meant to be.
Me a lesbian,
Why not? ▼

Coming Out to Dad
by Jennifer Anne Blair

I had a dilemma. I had started transitioning over nine months ago and had been living full time in my chosen gender role for about four months. At age 50 I was very fortunate to have been able to quit my job of 15 years prior to transitioning, so work wasn't an issue. As part of my real life experience I had enrolled in college and was taking a few classes in preparation of applying to graduate school in the next year or so. Transitioning involves many challenges and hurdles all of which I had been able to successfully conquer up until now. How do I tell my father?

My parents, who I am very close to, live in Florida and I live in Colorado. Both my mother and my father are in their late 70's and I hadn't seen them in a few years. It was very important to me to see them while I still had the opportunity. I had told all of my family members except Dad. Although my mother was a bit confused over the whole idea, she and my siblings had been very understanding and accepting of my choice. But when I brought up the idea of coming out to my father, the vote among my family was unanimous…"DON'T DO IT!"

My father was strict to a fault and ruled his roost with an iron fist. He was a "Man's Man" and placed very high value on living up to the unspoken code of conduct appropriate to the male gender. Throughout my childhood he had made a concerted effort to see to it that I carried on the time honored tradition of being "Manly". I had to agree with my family members that he was probably the last person on earth that would find my decision acceptable. My mother believed that at his age it could quite literally kill him. If it didn't kill him he would surely disown me. My mom suggested that I just try to pretend to be a boy for the week that I hoped to visit and let it go at that. Unfortunately it was too late for that. I had been on hormones for the last seven months, I'd had "ALL" of my body and facial hair permanently removed with laser and my now shoulder length hair put the finishing touches on what was now an unmistakably feminine appearance. Although I would have been willing to try to pretend to be a boy on his behalf, that was no longer a realistic option.

Although I was pretty sure I knew what she would say, I made an appointment with my psychologist to discuss the matter. She agreed that it really boiled down to only two possible options. I could keep my secret, as I had for most of my adult life and never see my parents again or roll the dice and hope for the best. As I had suspected these were the only two possibilities. For their 50-year-old son to merely show up at the airport as their daughter was not even a consideration. The latter would in all certainty result in a very emotional an regretfully ugly scene. More phone calls to my mother and siblings only strengthened their resolve to dissuade me from telling my father.

I spent weeks agonizing over this dilemma but to no avail. Over the last few months I had grown quite accustomed to explaining to friends and acquaintances that I was a transsexual in transition. For the most part this was no longer a choice but an obligation. When one shows up for their dentist appointment or sees an old friend at the grocery store wearing as skirt and blouse an explanation is generally forthcoming. I had also grown accustomed to finding myself quite favorably surprised by most of the responses. In spite of all of my fears and internalized transphobia most of these encounters turned out to be non-events! Once over the initial shock, most people responded with compassion and respect for my choice along with a genuine admiration for my courage…..but then there was Dad.

I still have no idea what came over me that day, I certainly had not planned on bring the subject up. While chatting with my parents on the phone, I said "Dad…I have something I need to tell you and you might want to sit down for this." My mother who already knew must have been at the brink of cardiac arrest at this point. "You're going to get married?" "Not exactly Dad." "You're moving to Florida?" "Come on Dad you know I hate hot weather." "Well then what is it?" About this time all I could think about was that baby picture they treasured…the one of me holding a football.

Over the course of the next 20 minutes or so I calmly and dispassionately explained the deep dark secret that I had carried with me over the course of the last 40+ years right down to the details of living full time and my hormone therapy. After I was done I took a long breath and waited for a response.

Anticipating a full on nuclear meltdown I was shocked to hear my father respond with equal impassivity and begin to ask a series of honest and genuinely sincere questions. Having gotten used to this drill by now I spent the next 45 minutes giving the usual course in transgender 101.

When we were done I gave a huge sigh of relief (along with my mother I'm sure). A moment that I had dreaded for so many years had come to a favorable conclusion. Within a matter of days BOTH of my parents were calling me Jennifer and referring to me as their daughter. I couldn't believe it Dad had accepted me! Needless to say the rest of my family was as shocked and amazed as I was. My greatest fear had turned out to be a non-event.

In retrospect it wasn't a non-event, it was actually quite eventful. Growing up I often suffered the brunt of my father's unpredictable and sometimes violent temper. I had spent most of my life fearing my father. This may sound cruel but up until that day I had never loved my father let alone respected him. Through the simple act of accepting me as my true self, compassionately and without reservation, he had earned my love and my respect. Thank you Dad.....I LOVE YOU. ▼

Jennifer would like to give special thanks to Dr. Rachael St. Claire, PsyD., her teacher, helper, mentor, guide and friend.

What Is Queer Pride?
by Stephen Collingsworth, Jr.

Well, first, let's start with what Queer Pride Isn't…

It isn't parties and dances where you shake your ass and have a good time, and heterosexuals come and gawk at all the queers, fun though that is.

It isn't chalkings that talk about "love," quote the bible, or tell people "we're here, we're queer, get over it", although that's fun too.

Queer pride isn't even about being proud that you sleep with, fall in love with, and share your life with someone of the same gender.

Queer pride isn't about a day, a week, a month, a parade, or any of those things.

Queer pride is about the small things. Every day living. Daring to live your life every day as an out gay, lesbian, bisexual, queer, transgendered, intersexual, omnisexual, pansexual, and all the other labels we choose to use to call ourselves different, person. Being unashamed of the totality of your self.

It's about looking at those you love and daring to share a part of you that may make them turn away from you.

It's about realizing that in order for your love of yourself, your parents, your friends, and/or your partner to grow and become fully realized, they all have to first know who you are.

It's realizing that Queerness isn't just about sex and whom you sleep with.

It's about looking at the world from the outside in.

It's about a clearer understanding of the world and how it ticks and what it needs to grow.

It's about realizing that our Queerness colors everything we do, see, smell, touch, learn, and feel.

It's about knowing you are NOT just like everyone else.

It's about being glad you are NOT just like everyone else.

Queer Pride is also about the journey; the journey from the closet into the light. It's about all of our paths from self-realization to sharing our completeness with others.

It is also about realizing our Queerness is a gift. And the sharing of that gift with others. It's about realizing that we are not the products of our parents. We are the inventors of ourselves... It's about our unique way of seeing the world differently and never seeing ourselves as static beings.

Queer pride is about reveling in our uniqueness, and to see that our uniqueness isn't all that unique! It's realizing there are others who are sharing a similar journey. Queer Pride is daring to love. Not finding that love in another person, no matter their gender. It's about daring to love yourself for who you are as an entire, whole person. ▼

*This submission is also available in poster format.
To purchase a poster please contact:
The Collegiate EmPowerment Company by calling toll free: 1-877-338-8246
or email: PosterInfo@Collegiate-EmPowerment.com. Posters also be viewed
and purchased online at: www.Collegiate-EmPowerment.com.
Thank you for your interest!

A Long Way From Ordinary
by Camille Perri

When the first daffodils bloom each spring, I think of my mom. Maybe it's because she always noticed things like that, the things too many people overlook. It was the beauty of the changing seasons that kept my mother going, even after the cancer came. And now, five years since she's been gone, every three months or so, when one season paves the way for the next, I am reminded to notice and take pleasure in the simple beauties of this world.

I like remembering those things. They don't hurt like so many other things do. They don't hurt the way it does to remember what happened to me and my mom after she found out she was sick and I figured out I was queer. Both occurred at just about the same time, and so we simultaneously became alienated from ourselves and one another. Separated by thin sheet rock walls and locked paneled doors, a monotone curse would leave our lips, the sigh of our failed normalcy and the lost simplicity of good health and straight privilege. Our bodies had betrayed us. She assumed she'd die of old age and I thought I'd marry the man of my dreams, I guess. But something inside both of us refused to cooperate with so typical an agenda.

Instead, I had a sick mother and she a daughter who looked like a son. Ghostlike voices haunted our minds, the result of years of conditioning, they whispered in our ears: Aren't mothers supposed to take care of daughters and not the other way around? And, aren't daughters supposed to become mothers and make grandmothers of their mothers? Isn't that the way it's supposed to be? Isn't that what's normal?

Deep down, we both resented the other for falling short of doing her job, for fucking up the precise structure of that pyramid, the one that plots each stage on the path to healthy adulthood. "Human Development," they call it, or some other catchy term that fits on the glossy pages of a high school Health textbook. That's where you learned the contents of a healthy, well-adjusted adult and the structure of a healthy, well-adjusted family.

Well, our pyramid had crumbled, leaving the supposed picture-perfect suburban household destroyed and in ruins. You see, our stages and roles were all mixed up and they didn't fit in the boxes or columns of the proper nuclear family, or any similar pyramided recipe for happiness. So we were miserable, well, we thought we should be miserable anyway, and so we were.

My mother and I hardly spoke for the entire last year of her life. Terrified by what her reaction to my queerness would be I pulled away and into my own introverted safety. She left me there, probably out of her own fear of finding out for sure what she didn't want to know but already could sense. When I did speak to her it was in anger, not at her directly but at her cancer, which I knew would leave me a motherless daughter. We both felt a bit cheated I suppose, cheated by life, and cheated by each other.

Sometimes expectations can overpower what's real. The concepts of constructed roles and responsibilities can make one forget that we're all just people. Not protocols, but people, who hurt, and need, and want, and fear, and get sick, and fall in love. Families don't fall apart because the people in them stop loving each other, but somehow they get tripped up on unrealistic ideals and fall apart anyway. My mom and I could have allowed our situation to bring us closer. Though completely different, her cancer and my queerness were the same in that they both challenged us to live our lives with a mark of distinction upon our foreheads, to face up to this world of regularity feeling anything but regular. But for us this was never confronted and the connections were never drawn and the resemblance never recognized. How could we have seen it when our eyes were blinded by the flashing neon propaganda telling us that being average is what we should have been striving for? It made us close our eyes and our minds and it hardened our hearts. Worst of all, it made us forget what real happiness is and what families really are, a group of people showing their love and letting themselves be loved.

Of course I didn't understand any of that while I was actually going through it. It has taken many sleepless nights with tears of guilt and regret streaming down my face to get to where I am today, but I feel that I'm a happier, more satisfied, person as a result of the journey. I don't think that I truly understood myself until after I began to search my soul for reasons and answers about why I acted the way I did when faced with my mother's illness and my newly discovered sexuality. That process of self-learning and understanding has not only allowed me to forgive myself but has taught me to love myself too. That is why I can now say that from my mother's life I learned to appreciate the beauty in nature and from my mother's death I learned to appreciate the beauty in myself, and in all of us. ▼

Tell Me
by David L Wallace

Tell me that there will be love
that lips will touch mine
that I will hold and be held
that the ache will recede from memory.

Tell me to wait
that intimacy cannot be hurried
that the hunger of desire is too quickly sated
that sparks must be fanned into flame.

Tell me that I will laugh
that joy will ravish me
that passion will destroy restraint
that bliss will shatter night's calm.

Tell me love's story
that I will take and be taken
that I will be exposed and embraced
that I will lie warm and secure.

Tell me that romance lives
that a shy smile will rend my heart
that the brush of soft skin will banish playful banter
that tender eyes will enfold mine.

Tell me that the search will end
that I will forget the pain of emptiness
that I will love, that I will rest.
Tell me that I am not a fool. ▼

Yes I Am
by Stephen Collingsworth

"Coming Out" has a myriad of meanings. It can mean admitting to oneself an attraction for members of the same gender. It can mean acting on those feelings in a physical way, or by taking part in social situations such as clubs, organizations, bars or shops. It can mean being out to oneself, to one's friends, to one's family, or in one's workplace. It can and does mean any, all, or a combination of these things. Coming Out is a lifelong process. Not a one time deal, much as we may wish it. Coming Out is perpetual growth into understanding who one is and the possibilities of the life we live.

Many heterosexuals ask, "why Come Out?" It's not easy to Come Out to oneself. We have all heard the jokes, the hurtful stereotypes, and the horrendous myths that circulate about LGBT people. Society tends to hate or fear that which it does not understand. It's very tempting to hide in the closet. But the closet is a painful and lonely place to be, even if the reason you stay is survival. It takes a lot of energy to deny feelings, and it is often costly. Many LGBT people turn to alcohol or other drugs to numb themselves against the pain society inflicts. Many consider and attempt suicide.

LGBT people do not Come Out to hurt their families and friends. We Come Out to begin healing the hurt society inflicts upon us. We Come Out to affirm and assert our worth as human beings first to ourselves, and then to others. The vast majority of LGBT people report feeling "a weight being lifted" from their shoulders.

Admitting that you actually are what many in society think is the worst thing to call you can be a rather cathartic experience.

"What you do in bed is your own business." Not true. What I do in bed *should* be my business. Unfortunately, society insists on making it their business and passes laws to restrict our relationships. Society deems what we do in bed as legal or illegal, whether or not our relationships have merit and meaning, and concerns itself in deciding if we should be parents.

In most of the United States, we can be fired from our jobs, kicked out of our apartments, denied bank loans, and be turned out of stores and restaurants because of our sexual orientation. In Coming Out we begin the process of taking back control of our own lives. Rather than sitting back meekly and allowing others to dictate how we should live our lives, we begin finding our voices as individuals. Those two small words, "I Am," contain the seeds that, with nurturing, can grow a healthy, vibrant, empowered, and productive individual able to contribute to the betterment of society.

Coming Out is a very personal, complicated process. And one that should not be entered into lightly. After you utter those two powerful words, "I Am," it is veritably impossible to take them back. Parents have been known to disown their children, kick them out into the street, cut them off financially. Churches, temples and synagogues have removed members of their congregation. Friends have turned their backs. People you once knew, loved, trusted, and depended on may become strangers. "National Coming Out Day" is not meant for everyone to get up and announce to the world "Yes I Am." Only those who have the strength to do so. For others, it is meant to encourage you to begin the life journey. If you can't proclaim yourself publicly, perhaps you are ready to admit it to yourself privately.

As for me, "Yes I Am." And you know what? I'm glad I am. In being so, I have learned the joys of unconditional love, of empathy, and of accepting and appreciating humanity in all its infinite, wondrous variety. I am who I am because of this journey. And I am enjoying the ride. ▼

Awakening
by Raul Medina

Are You a Boy or a Girl?
by Gabriel Hermelin

I can't keep track of how many times a child has asked me that question, in public no less, like while waiting in line to buy popcorn at the movies or in the restroom at a shopping center. My usual answer is, "both", which immediately confuses the poor child and causes their parent to grab them by the arm and drag them off.

I don't remember exactly when I realized that my gender expression was not what people thought it ought to be, but I do remember when people starting hassling me about being a, "Dyke". I was 16 years old. At the time I had long hair, so I'm not sure why they called me sir, but they did, and it pissed me off. I was insulted. I wanted to be called by my name or nothing at all. Somewhere along the way in my life I had learned the lesson that being a "tomboy" was supposed to end at adolescence. It didn't. And I was afraid when people called me names, so I fought against the stereotype of lesbian equals want-to-be-a-man and refused to acknowledge the transgender nature within me. I was afraid to be different, even if it was within the LGBT community or rather yet the gay and lesbian community as it was called.

Being lesbian-identified as a young person, I was convinced that I had to be either a femme or a butch, but I was both. I had to be aggressive or passive, but I was both. I had to be weak or strong, but I was both. I was and still am a blend of feminine and masculine energies, expressing emotions and charting my course through life with great strides. Is that anti-feminine? Is that anti-masculine? In a society that puts people into categories of male/female, masculine/feminine, aggressive/passive, based on sex assignment at birth, it sure looks that way.

What was it about me that gave the impression of maleness? Was it my clothes, which were loose and comfortable? Was it that I was in relationships with women and only men were allowed to do that? Was it that I was confidant and made eye contact with people when I walked in public? Was it that I had a loud voice and I was constantly using it to champion for LGBT rights? Who knows why and who cares. I was comfortable with who I was, but at the time I was unaware of a transgender movement or community.

As a young person I knew that there were men who wore clothes considered to be women's and that some even went through surgery and took hormones to be women, but I never knew that there were women out there who dressed like men, passed as men and became men. Now, I don't want to be a "man", or a "woman" for that matter, not if they come with rigid roles, but I am grateful to the FtM, Female-to-Male, community for their courage and presence, because now I feel able to express myself, along the gender continuum, without reservation and proudly proclaim, "I am a tranny queer!". ▼

If Only...
by Shane L. Windmeyer

If only... my Mom would not had dressed me up as a girl when I was less than one year old. I mean it was a lovely white dress with a dainty pink bow tied in my hair. My dimples and rosy cheeks were a curse. All the women poking and squeezing. I guess, that's probably what made me gay -- the dimples, rosy cheeks, the dress, the pink bow, the women poking and squeezing.

If only... I would not have gone to the "family" doctor. We all know what that means, "family," it's the gay recruitment term along with rainbows and lollipops. I mean it must be something the doctor gave me when I was a kid, possibly a GTB (gay testosterone booster) or he activated an OGG (obviously gay gene). Surely, it was the Doc that made me gay?

If only... I had not grown up on a small farm in the middle of Kansas -- full of cows, chickens, pigs, the whole barnyard. I mean I was doomed with Bob Dole as my senator and all the friends of Dorothy and rainbows everywhere. Click, click, click those heels and say three times "there's no place like homo..." The Land of Oz and all the beefy farm boys surely made me gay, right?

If only... I had not been so active in Boy Scouts and Cub Scouts. You know all those overnight camping trips with other boys, the festive beads, colorful badges, the handmade ornaments, and you can't forget the snazzy neckerchiefs adorned with a gold or silver bolo tie... come on, the Boy Scouts did not make me gay, did it?

If only... my interests in college were not theatre, art and music. You know all that life is a stage business, the dancing, costumes, makeup, hmmmmm.... I love show tunes to death and "Evita" is one of my favorite musicals turned movie with Madonna, of course. I know all the classical names -- Janet, Cher, Babs, Christina, Britney, Celine, Whitney before Bobby Brown and do not forget the boy band, NSYNC. Maybe pop culture made me gay?

If only... I was better at sports... because we all know that a touchdown, grand slam, and three point shot is a sure way to be straight. Right? Hmmmm... maybe not, I forgot about Troy, Daryl, Glenn, Mike, Joey. Oh my and how could I forget the swim team. I think the sweat, adrenaline and all the tight uniforms made us gay...

If only... I had avoided the one gay guy on campus who was out. He cross-dressed in skirts with striped colorful hosiery and rode a bike across campus that had a basket on the front with shiny tassels. He carried this black box with metal bolts riveted around the sides that read "BOY TOY." I should have dashed the other way when I saw him coming my way. Surely, he convinced me to be gay.

If only... I did not join a fraternity; this is it for sure... right? All the late night jock runs, the brotherhood bonding, formal dinners with all men and do not forget touch football games on Sundays -- I am sure that joining a fraternity gave me the "gaybees." Where else can you get it in such a high dose in college?

If only... my girlfriend was not the one that turned every guy she knew gay. I mean who would guess the football team captain was gay. You know, I figured it all out, she had this secret power beyond gaydar, I'm sure. Her objective to rid the world of the nemesis, "straight men." Whatever guy she touched turned gayer than an Abercrombie & Fitch department store. Was my girlfriend really a gay superhero named "SheGAY" who sent gay vibes out to the most unsuspecting men? Watch out, it's SheGAY! Did she change me?

If only… GAP did not have such cool, hip clothing and such hot male employees to recruit, I mean fold the clothes. I mean surely the spiked hair, muscular build, tan and did I say "hottie" GAP employee made me gay. Mesmerizing me with his folding routine of worn denim pants to forest green polos to cocoa chocolate colored v-necks to ribbed crew necks to pokka-dot boxers to their ever-so-stylish khakis… I mean where does it stop! It is the straight man's worst nightmare – style, neatness and coordination all in one. And, least we not forget the sub-liminal message of the name GAP – Gay And Proud! I know it has to be the GAP that made me stylish, hip and maybe gay?

If only… I would have avoided eye contact with the guy at the university fitness center. You know him. Screen name: muscjck21 Stats: All American, 6 foot something, 180 lbs, muscular build; 46c; 17a; 32w; crew cut; blue eyes, smooth hard pecs…you get the idea. He was too perfect to be straight. I mean he was at least bisexual. I'm sure he did me in after we went out that one time. It was too tempting not to be gay then...

If only… I would not have joined the Gay and Straight Alliance on campus. I was merely trying to support my friends and be an ally. I enjoyed participating in the "Guess Who's Straight" speak-er panels, the dances, the parties… Maybe it was those rainbow colored cookies I ate that first night or the handshake from the co-presidents. I wonder who won the toaster when I became gay?

If only… I were straight than I would not be gay. I believe that we all live in a world of "if only" at some point in our life, whether we are straight or gay. Always desiring to be the opposite, to have something more, to be something better, to be accepted, to be something we are not. I used to think that I wanted to be straight all the time, before I figured out what made me gay. It was not my Mom dressing me up as a baby in a pink bow and letting the women poke and squeeze my dimples, rosy cheeks that made me gay. Nope! It was not the family doc, Boy Scouts, "SheGay" the superhero, muscjck21 or my fraternity brothers for that matter either... No Sireee!

If only... you were gay. Maybe, you are, than you already know the answer to the mystery, what makes me gay? It comes from within... like a bag of rainbow colored Skittles waiting to be gobbled up... like wanting to vote for the pink M&M even though you know it will clash with the green ones... like laughing out loud when this "too straight tough" guy says "that's so gay" to fit in on campus. Who is he fooling, right? You know, you know already what makes me gay.

It has happened to me every day of my life. From the moment I was born a baby, the kisses, hugs and caring support of my mom, dad and sister made me gay. The love that my partner Tom and I share for one another, did it too! All my family and friends that make us proud of who we are and stand by us, definitely had something to do with it. God made me gay, no doubt. Even my neighbors and my community make me gay. I am blessed every day to be gay and it is now obvious what made me gay, isn't it?

What made me gay... is who *I am.* ▼

*This submission is also available in poster format.
To purchase a poster please contact:
The Collegiate EmPowerment Company by calling toll free:
1-877-338-8246 or email:
PosterInfo@Collegiate-EmPowerment.com.
Posters also be viewed and purchased online at:
www.Collegiate-EmPowerment.com.
Thank you for your interest!

The Strong Ones
by Emily Rokosch

I am a swimmer for a Division I program. There seems to be a lot of homophobia centered around Division I athletics. My experiences as an open lesbian on a Division I collegiate program have been nothing but the best.

It has been said one must be strong and at times even courageous to live out an openly gay or lesbian lifestyle. I can agree with that, but for me, it is my swim team who are the courageous ones, it is my swim team who are the strong ones......

Sitting at a restaurant, they ask without a whisper or a hushed voice how my girlfriend is doing.....
they are the strong ones.

Walking through a video and CD store, they tell me I should not put up with bad customer service just because I asked for a lesbian themed movie.....
they are the strong ones.

During the swim meets, they are the ones who ask if I am going to bring my rainbow towel, and smile at me when the big bright flag is on the side of the pool.....
they are the strong ones.

In classes, if discriminating comments are said against gays and lesbians, they speak up, they correct the language.....
they are the strong ones.

When their parents come to visit, they are not ashamed that I am a lesbian, they do not change their words.....
they are the strong ones.

When rainbow ribbons are handed out on National Coming Out Day, they put them on their bulletin boards, they wear them on their book bags.....
they are the strong ones.

When I attend AIDS rallies or pride celebrations, they are by my side, they are clapping and raising their hands.....
they are the strong ones.

When I am tired, when I can not smile, when I wonder why it is sometimes so hard to be me...they are my shoulders to lean on, my arms to cry in, my voice to speak with, and my faces to smile with.....*They Are The Strong Ones.* ▼

*This submission is also available in poster format.
To purchase a poster please contact:
The Collegiate EmPowerment Company by calling toll free: 1-877-338-8246
or email: PosterInfo@Collegiate-EmPowerment.com. Posters also be viewed
and purchased online at: www.Collegiate-EmPowerment.com.
Thank you for your interest!

Virgin Lesbian Straight Up
by Noelle Messier

"Virgin Lesbian," hmmm..., sounds like a newfangled cocktail. Hey Bartender, get me a Virgin Lesbian on the rocks. On second thought, make that a Virgin Lesbian with a twist. Better yet, a Virgin Lesbian Sour – hold the cherry please.

Humor is often the easiest way to deal with unfamiliar explorations into the unknown. I guess the journey begins with my attraction to one particular bartender. She had the most beautiful blue eyes I'd ever seen.

A little background on my sexuaity. I've always considered myself heterosexual. I had a boyfriend in the third grade. I remember one hot day in the library when he sneaked up behind me and kissed me on the back of my head. So soft and sweet. I kept telling him I couldn't feel it through my hair to get him to repeat this ecstasy over and over again. My first french kiss was in fifth grade; Good old spin the bottle. I thought I'd died and gone to heaven. I dated through high school and college. My longest relationship with a man was two years, six months. Most lasted two weeks or less. Sometimes just two hours before I knew it would never last; so what was the point.

Lurking in the background, since college really, was this strange electric feeling I'd get every now and again in the presence of certain women. I remember one particular friend of mine in college who got me all hot and bothered just knowing I would see her that day. These feelings always came and went without incident. Particularly because they were always with straight women. And of course I was straight myself; so what was the point.

Lesbian scenes in movies always got my fluids moving. Since,

"Even Cowgirl's Get the Blues," I haven't been able to look at Uma Thurman quite the same way. So, I guess there were signs. I had just chosen to ignore them.

So, into my life walks Raven, my bartender friend. (Soap opera names have been used to protect the innocent.) Raven was my first female friend who dated women. I'm purposely avoiding using labels here; such as, lesbian or bisexual, because frankly they still confuse the heck out of me. After hanging out a few times I admitted I had never dated a woman but wasn't opposed to the idea in theory. The opportunity had just never come up.

I'm an actress who had just completed two years of Meisner acting training in NYC. Which is basically, intense, gut wrenching, emotional self discovery, tied to a brilliant acting technique. I had also been exploring spiritual new age healing and energy work. So, I guess you could say, I had become pretty open minded and it was getting more and more difficult to keep my emotions bottled up, hidden deep within my hard shell. My emotions were no longer a curse to be denied, but a blessing to be celebrated and expressed. A beautiful flower had been growing inside of me and it was time to allow it to bloom.

Raven began to inspire sexual feelings in me I never knew existed. I would just think about her and this intense tingling energy would shoot through me like a water spout. I thought gee... this must be love. I've never felt anything this powerful. I suddenly understood all the love songs. I was so energized and turned on I didn't know what to do with myself. I was enraptured with this wonderful thrill of a feeling.

Writing it wasn't quite enough. The thought needed to be expressed whether I liked it or not.

One click of the e-mail button and the message was sent.

Did I mention that Raven has a girlfriend named Brook? Swept up in my emotional intoxication I had kind of ignored that fact. Too late. Raven got my e-mail and its implications. She was shocked, surprised, and very flattered. However; the fact remained, she had a girlfriend. Case closed.

This situation put quite a strain on our friendship. It felt awkward for her to talk about Brook. Sometimes I chose to completely ignore Brook's existence and lose myself in romantic fantasy. At other times, painful reality was inescapable. I was so frightened of this deep love inside of me and yet so exhilarated at the same time. The thought of loosing this newly discovered feeling was devastating.

By some small miracle we remained friends through this ordeal. Raven helped me to discover a very important thing. All of these feelings weren't about her at all. This rapturous energy wasn't emanating from her, but from me. An urge that had been repressed for too long. The water pressure had been building. The hose burst and happened to spray the closest lesbian in proximity. What was stirring wasn't love for Raven; but, a love for all women. In a way it was me opening up to love of all humankind. As my dear male friend, Trenton, said "Just think you've increased your odds of finding true love by 50%. How great is that?"

With my new found freedom I was ready to go exploring. The biggest lesbian tea dance of the year was happening at Tavern on the Green the night before Thanksgiving. My family was celebrating Thanksgiving on Friday, the day after Thanksgiving, because it was the only time we could all get together. Although, I felt like a turkey about to enter the slaughter house. I was meeting Raven, her girlfriend, and some mutual acquaintances at the dance. I entered Tavern on the Green with all it's brilliant blue Christmas lights and headed down a seemingly endless hallway.

I walked into this incredible endless sea of pulsating women. It was another world and the makings of a great soap opera. This ocean was full of fragile sea horses with trussed up angel fish; lanky sea cucumbers attached to their stocky, strong rocks; sparkling star fish wanting all the attention; sea anemones, complete with big hair (I think they were from Brooklyn); and ,of course, the sharks were everywhere. What's a frightened guppy to do? Well, I kept swimming, trying to ignore the enjoyment I was getting accidentally rubbing up beside a bunch of octopuses. I found my friends clinging to a sandbar in the corner of the room.

I had the time of my life. There's an incredible energy of freedom and acceptance you feel in a room with that many women all dancing to the same beat. I even have to say I liked Raven's girlfriend. I danced most of the night with an acquaintance I knew from work. Her name was Chase. Dancing with Chase was like dancing with an electric eel. Her body was everywhere and when we touched, the electricity flowed through me like a bolt of lightening. I guess you could say the sea had parted and I knew life would never be the same again.

So, where am I now? Well, I might be still attracted to men. I don't know. But, this woman thing seems so much more intense. I'm not dating either at the moment. I am still yet to experience my first lesbian kiss; I know I want to though. So, am I a virgin lesbian? Or a bisexual virgin lesbian? I don't know. What I do know is that I have a lot to learn. My journey is just beginning. But most importantly; I now know that it's okay to allow myself to love and to express that wondrous part of me in whatever form it takes. After all, isn't that what makes life interesting?

So Bartender; I guess I'll take that Virgin Lesbian........ to go! ▼

Someone Else's Life
by Lissa Guillet

Dawn Breaks.
The alarm awakens.
Another day begins.
The mirror lies.
A chained image,
Concealed beneath her skin.

Her heart breaks,
Her soul shatters,
Inside her current guise,
As she watches
A life go by
Through her tear-filled eyes.

Boys don't cry.
Boys don't fear
To live their lives as men.
But little girls
Betray themselves
When told they don't fit in.

His tears stop.
His face dries.
He shuts away her strife.
Her mind, her heart, Her childhood lost
In someone else's life.

Another day begins... ▼

Embracing the Girly-Boy Within
by R Perry Monastero

I remember skipping alongside my father at age three by an empty baseball field. I craned my neck up and said, "You wanted a boy first, dinchya'." He turned, scrunched his eyes trying to discern what his first-born just said.

You see, I was born physically a boy, but my problem fitting in was that I possessed the stereotypical characteristics of both sexes. In nursery school, I often played the Mommy in the game "House" out in the schoolyard. It came naturally and I enjoyed it as much as playing Dad. However, playing Mommy got me in a little bit of trouble. Teachers chastised me with gender-appropriateness lectures and forced me to sit inside for recess until I wanted to be more masculine. "Harumph!" I thought, mimicking my finicky grandmother, Nana Bailey. By the way, Nana's name is Dorothy and she's from Kansas. She was an orphan raised by her aunt and uncle and lived on a rural farm. As a little girl, she had a black Terrier, enjoyed singing, and had gorgeous red hair. And, if Judy Garland were alive today, they'd be the same age! I'm serious.

Now, in first grade, I further learned the butch-it-up-boy lesson when Matthew McSomething-or-another and I decided to get married. He was so sweet, but my folks were non-plussed. Dad said, "Son, you can't do that in Pennsylvania . . . though some Xerox guys I know did that in California." Mom said, "Now go, run and play." Soon after, Matthew talked about exchanging rings. Over dinner I insisted on having a thick gold band with a bright red ruby. After Matthew left, Mom and Dad were having none of that. So, I promptly locked myself in my room, had a tempter tantrum, and taped a note to my door (I was precocious at six) that read "I will stay in my room until I can have a gold ring." Meanwhile, I lay under my covers and fantasized about turning the heads of older boys by struttin' my stuff along the park sidewalk.

Now, I wonder just where is that Matthew boy these days?!

I was always a busy kid. Yeah, and I liked to do girl things and boy things. More than half of my friends were always girls, but you would find me equally at home with the guys getting my boots muddy in the creek or constructing dirt bike trails through the woods. I played with toy cars and planes but constantly broke Mother's sacred "no men in the kitchen" rule by baking cakes. I swam competitively and broke a couple of records here and there, all the while having hidden crushes on boys in the next age group above. At 14, I twinkled a flowery Tchaikovsky (a big Mary) concerto for recital crowds and joined the Boy Scouts, Post #200 in Fairfield, Connecticut. Here's a little something special for the U.S. Supreme Court: I was in a troop that had co-ed tents. It wasn't until a reunion ten years later that I learned one of my scoutmasters was a lesbian who had adopted two children with her partner.

I played sports most of my life. Growing up, I kicked some major butt on the soccer field. Above all, I loved soccer on a warm fall day after a good rain and practicing diving headers into the goal. I'm thinking I'm part lesbian. A lipstick lesbian, perhaps. I guess right about now it feels good to admit that I dabbled a little with Mom's cosmetics.

[Uh, Mom? Cat's outta the bag now. You didn't notice, did ya'?]

In fifth grade my entire class ostracized me so badly that Mrs. Jones demanded I "stop taunting the others by being so . . ."

and then she'd sigh deeply because I knew she could not say the word 'gay.' I just stared at her unable to speak as the tears welled up and choked my throat. It didn't make sense.

Mrs. Sloan, my junior high guidance director set me straight, so to speak. I was the problem, I learned. She once pulled me into her office along with Keith, the most popular guy in school. She asked Keith to explain "why Perry gets picked on." Keith glared and said, "Perry rhymes with 'fairy.' Ignore it and it will all go away." And with that, Mrs. Sloan agreed and asked us to leave. Tell me now, who can ignore an entire cafeteria chanting "Faggot!" or a gym class screaming "Fairy"? After all the chasing, shoves, punches, and threats, I learned to butch it up.

We moved a bunch and with each subsequent transfer, the threat of girly-boy or gay-bashing remained. I learned how to hide my true two-gender self better and better. And, I buried a big part of my soul in the process. Most regrettably, the torture was hardest on the soccer field. The fears eventually scared me into giving up every extracurricular organization.

Enter college. The first month I experienced daily gay-bashing and threats, which I kept to myself. I quickly powered more energy into fitting in more than I had ever done. And I excelled at what I call "passing for straight-living." I dated girls, became fraternity president, and lead student government. People were nicer because of my status, yet I always sensed that most saw through my 'pseudo-enhanced' masculinity.

One day a major realization crashed down while my best friend Josh and I watched "The Ambiguously Gay Duo" on Saturday Night Live (I'm sooo not kidding here). The cartoon made us laugh our asses off, especially at the sight of the tandem-flying duo holding one other, (cough), albeit ambiguously. Here were two TV cartoon gay guys doing their athletic thing and being comedic heroes about it. I know this sounds hokey, but, it's all true. Reader, you still with me? I cried non-stop and after an hour finally told Josh how I felt as a girly-boy.

I had no clue at that time how and where I could go to re-enter the world of sports. Consequently, I started coming out to more friends and cousins. Then I told my parents and more friends and co-workers. Soon after my emotional well-breaking I found myself in the midst of HOTGUY4Us, 3some4NOWs, and BIstud69ers in an online chat room. That's where I met AndyZ151. (OK, okay, my name was Spanks Junior). Turns out Andy had a lot of interesting things to say. Also turns out that Andy had joined the same fraternity from another campus and lived in my Dad's old stompin' grounds. We talked about his job and mine. Hee hee. I'm laughing to myself right about now 'cuz I just remembered my County Commissioner Republican Godfather promoted gay Andy in the public defender's office.

Anyhoo, Andy talked about playing soccer and it struck a major chord. I wanted to get back into it, too, but how could I? He gave me all the details and then added the kicker – the team was historically gay, and there were hundreds of LGBTQ sports teams in the country, many more in the world for that matter. I was dumbfounded. I had to know more.

In a matter of weeks Andy and I became fast friends and the soccer captain visited my house. I was sold on the team and gained the confidence to come back to something I had sorely missed. I found the first place of many more to follow where I could learn to reintegrate my diverged and submerged identity.

And thus, this is how I came out in two ways: as a girly-boy and a gay man. So, ya' wanna play some ball with me?

I'm talkin' about soccer, silly. ▼

A Letter from a Mother of a 17 Year Old Male-to-Female Transexual Child to Family and Friends

Dearest Family and Friends,

My husband and I are purchasing a house in Charlestown so that David and I will have a place to start a new journey.

The journey actually started for me around eight months ago when David came to me and told me that before the age of five years old he has felt uncomfortable about his body. He felt that he should have been born a girl. He did not like these feeling as they made him feel confused, sad and lonely.

Imagine a little boy, your little boy laying in bed at night praying to God to please let him wake up the next day a little girl and correct the mistake that was made at birth. Not a pleasant thought.

Well, he continues to feel that everything about his life is wrong and that he can no longer live the lie that he has been living for the past 17 years. His discomfort level with his body is such, that he has tried to commit suicide on more than one occasion and he will do so if he is forced to live a life that does not conform with his mind, his soul and his spirit.

Through the years, to counteract and hopefully change his feeling of being a girl, David has tried desperately to change his mental image of himself. He played football, baseball, high school track, ice and roller hockey. He tried so hard that he excelled in all. He finished his hockey career with the award for the most valuable goalie in the national competition held in Iowa. He felt the rougher the sport the less chance anyone would find out about his secret.

You see not only is Gender Identity Disorder devastating to the individuals sense of well being but it is the shame one feels that is the hardest part to endure. It is the shame that society puts on the individual that they feel does not conform to the so-called "norms".

The ironic part of this is that the professionals feel that this disorder is biological in nature. So all this shame for what? David has no control over this feeling. Oh course, it is not a choice regardless of what the causes are. In order to get any kind of relief from this gender dysphoria, the person must either commit suicide, resign to live a lie and be totally miserable for life or have sex reassignment surgery. Not something that sounds like a choice to me.

Being the parents that Bob and I are, we have chosen to use our unconditional love to show David that he will not be destined to a life of misery. He will have everything that is possible to make his life easier and happier than even he could have imagined in those dark and lonely nights that he spent in the dark crying and praying for a miracle that could never happen. It took David an incredible amount of courage and 16 years of his life to ask for the help and understanding that is needed to start the long and difficult transition to become the person that David was destined to become.

Well, this brings me back to the journey that David and I am about to embark. Once we start this trip there is no turning back. I say we because I will be with David every step of the way. Just like I would be if he had cancer or any other devastating illness. I will not rest until I see my sweet David transformed into the girl that she so desires I understand that this will take you some time getting used to, and I will be happy to talk over with you any questions or thoughts you may have about any of this, but please don't feel sorry for us. Yes, we are facing a difficult situation but not one that is expected to end in death or some other sad scenario. We look at this as if a butterfly was about to spread its wings. A beautiful living creature is going from being trapped in a dreadful dark existence to a lovely bright being.

I understand that you may question the resolution that we have chosen but in my hours and hours of research, and my meetings with the professionals there is no "cure". Or is there a chance that these feelings will ever go away. Nothing will ever change this, except change.

So, my dear friends and family, what I am asking from you is compassion and understanding of something that you may never understand. I am asking that you look into the eyes of your loved ones and cherish the important things in life and not get caught up in the "little" things, because we never know what the very next minute may bring to our lives.

One other thing I ask is to please don't treat us like lepers; we are very comfortable talking about this to anyone. We have educated ourselves enough to answer any question you may have about Gender Identity Disorder. We are not embarrassed about this and we hope that you will not be with us either. We did not ask for this to happen but with any other challenge that God gives us, we pick up our cross and bear it. If we can make you feel any more comfortable about it, please let us help you.

With a Loving Heart,
Louise ▼

My Friend, My Brother
by George Miller

Ken and I were really looking forward to the upcoming weekend. Earlier in the week, I had called him and convinced him to go on a road trip with me. We were excited because our fraternity was hosting our annual Maze Party, one of the biggest weekends of the year. Like us, many alumni would be back in town and we were excited about seeing our old friends. Still, I had another reason to be anxious…

Four years earlier I was a sophomore sitting in the chapter room of the Sigma Alpha Epsilon house with the rest of my brothers. We were finishing up spring rush and were meeting to discuss the potential members. Things were moving along pretty quickly until we got to one particular candidate. Ken was a second semester freshman and was liked by many of the members. On paper, he was an exceptional candidate. Some of the brothers, though, had concerns about other aspects of Ken.

Ken is African-American. At that time, we had no African-American members, and had never had any, according to our knowledge. A couple of brothers said that they wanted to keep alive the tradition of our very southern fraternity and not give a bid to a black student. In addition to his race, other brothers were in turmoil about a rumor they had heard about Ken. Many were thinking it and finally one brother raised his hand and asked, "Is Ken gay?" Andy and Trael, two brothers who knew Ken best, declared that there was no truth to the rumor. While some were still concerned, we took a vote and the majority of the membership was in favor of Ken.

Ken was the final candidate up for vote and everyone started to gather their things as our business was done. Before anyone left though, Andy and Trael said that they needed to address the chapter. The uneasy look on their faces told us that they had something important to say. Andy and Trael confessed that Ken was indeed gay. They had promised Ken that they would not let his sexuality be an issue in the chapter's decision to extend him a bid. Although they had lied to the chapter, they had honored their promise to Ken.

Many of the brothers were visibly upset, not so much with what Andy and Trael had done, but that we now were forced to reconsider our decision. Many of the brothers including myself grew up in rural Midwestern farm towns. We didn't have much exposure to racially or ethnically diverse people, let alone some-one who was homosexual. The idea of having a gay brother was difficult for many on a personal level because of their religious beliefs. Others were concerned about our chapter's image. Would we be labeled the "gay house" on campus? If others found out about Ken, would it hurt us in rush? Over the next few hours many tears were shed and harsh words exchanged. In the end, we decided to honor the decision we had made earlier in the night. It was almost 5 o'clock in the morning and we were emotionally exhausted. In retrospect, I don't think I've ever been more proud of my chapter.

The next day Ken accepted his bid into our brotherhood. Over the next few weeks, we all got to know him and realized that we had made the right decision. Even the biggest homophobes in the chapter grew to love him as their brother. Over the next couple of years Ken continued to be an outstanding student leader. He was always the life of the party and one of the most well-liked students on campus. The chapter's concerns about rush were completely unfounded; Ken was the recipient of our

"Outstanding Rusher" award two years in a row. Ken and I were both Orientation Leaders for the University and we became great friends through our involvement with that program as well as the fraternity. Several times during his college career, brothers took Ken aside and told him how much they valued him as a brother and how much they had learned from him. I honestly think he was the best thing that ever happened to our chapter. When I left Indiana for graduate school, I knew that he would be one of the people I would miss most.

Riding with Ken that weekend, four years later, I had a knot in my stomach. I told him there was another reason I was going to Evansville. Ken's response was, "George, who's the girl?" I said, "Ken, there is no girl. But, I do have two things that I want to tell you. First of all, I want to apologize to you. Even though we've been friends for four years, I haven't been as supportive of you as I could have been. Although I always passed them off as jokes, on several occasions I've made offensive remarks about your sexuality. Sometimes you've been around to hear them and sometimes you haven't. I'm sorry if my comments have ever caused you to feel bad about yourself."

Ken said that he appreciated my apology and that it was no big deal. He had gotten used to the jokes and didn't let them get to him. Then he asked, "So what's the second thing you have to tell me?"

I said, "The second thing I want to tell you is 'thank you."

Ken said, "for what?"

I said, "I want to thank you for not apologizing for who you are. I want to thank you for not compromising your values. I want to thank you for walking down the street with your head held high. I want to thank you for giving me the courage to able to verbalize what I've known in my heart for a long time. I'm gay too. Last weekend I came out to a handful of brothers who were visiting Florida for spring break. They were so supportive that I decided to come up to Evansville this weekend to tell the rest. Without you as a role model, I would never have had the courage to do it."

We had a great time that weekend. Although it was difficult at first, I ended up coming out to my fraternity brothers and other friends who were in town that weekend. They have all been very supportive of me, just like I hoped they would be. I have Ken to thank for that. I was 23 years old before I could say what Ken had said back in high school. Pessimists will tell you that one person can't make a difference. Obviously, they haven't met my friend, my brother, Ken. ▼

Inalienable Rights
by Margo Browall

Well, I got the third degree again today
from someone conditioned by the masses
to believe the way I love is wrong.

His brutal line of questioning
left me bruised and insulted and mad as hell
that I must constantly prove my right to belong.

If a choice has been made
it's to live free
to be me
and I won't apologize.
Those inalienable rights
apply to me as much as you

What would you have me do?

I could lie, I could live an illusion
with someone who was unaware
going through the motions
masking desperate emotions
pretending that I care

Where is the humanity in that?

In your brainwashed mind you've been led to believe
that I have the problem, but you've been deceived
and you think I would choose to forge a lonely path
down the road of my life, risking society's wrath

Where is the logic in that?

If a choice has been made
it's to live free
to be me
and I won't apologize.
Those inalienable rights
apply to me as much as you.

Too often I find I must defend
myself from a hatred that has no end.
You say you want what's best for me--
as long as it fits your philosophy.

But I choose to live free, to be me!
I won't apologize. ▼

*This submission is also available in poster format.
To purchase a poster please contact:
 The Collegiate EmPowerment Company by calling toll free:
1-877-338-8246 or email: PosterInfo@Collegiate-EmPowerment.com.
Posters also be viewed and purchased online at:
www.Collegiate-EmPowerment.com. Thank you for your interest!

The Inspiration Book Series

Betrayed
by Lisa M. Hartley

(Please Note: "I" refers to a voice from the transgender community and "You" refers to culture, which includes all of us.)

I was betrayed. Betrayed by you and betrayed unto myself. For half a century I struggled without understanding, without hope, without help. Now I know. Now I'm free. I share my knowledge with you, but still you betray me. You push me into the margins of society. You don't see me when I'm near. To you, I am invisible. To you, I am less than I was before. Somehow my victory in becoming the real me has offended you. You think I'm crazy. You think I'm gay. You think all kinds of things, almost all of which is steeped in a kind of mythology, reflective of your fear. You deny me a place. You deny me meaningful work. You take away my standing and greet me with a jaundiced eye.

Strangely, I still love you. I still want to share my story with you. I still need you. I don't want to be alone any more. So please listen to me. Listen with an open mind and an open heart. This is what happened.

When I was born, the doctor looked at my genitals and said, "it's a boy." He didn't know that I was both. I looked like a boy between my legs, but in my head, the place that defines the sex that I really am, I was a girl. The doctor couldn't see inside my head, nor could anyone else. So they named me Billy.

You taught me to be a boy. I didn't know any better until I was four. I didn't like being a boy. But I was told I was by every measure. So I hid my thoughts and dreams inside. It was my cross to bear. My hell. You induced this stress on me that I would struggle with for decades.

There were many barriers and many mazes in my journey. I wondered if I was crazy, if I was gay, if my hormones or genetics were messed up, or if I would ever get over the feeling that I was "different" from everybody else.

But then I read an article in the November 1995 issue of Nature magazine that changed my life. It said that I was right to want to be a lady. My brain revealed the answer to the mystery. My brain was female! The genitals were only incidental. Although they looked normal and behaved that way, my genitals reflected another sex, different from my brain. I was born with two sex identities. Yet only one can be primary, according to the body's need for balance, i.e. homeostasis.

A book by John Colapinto entitled "As Nature Made Him," talked about David Reimer's surgical sex assignment from male to female after a botched circumcision. When he realized the betrayal, David would not live as a female. His brain confirmed his true sex identity that was, in fact, male.

In May 2000 a study was reported, that focused on intersexed babies, born with incomplete genitalia. Although surgical sex identity assignment to female was done on 25 babies, 14 of them demanded to be male. The genitals proved to be incidental to sex identity. But the sex identity reflected in the brain, ruled.

It seems to me, that the truth revealed by scientific research, i.e. that the brain is primary in sex identity, and confirmed by all the heartbreaking, pain-filled life experience stories told by transgendered persons, that the truth about transgender would finally be heard and accepted by everyone. But you scoffed at the anecdotal stories, dismissing them as folklore. You ignored the scientific findings. You tightened your grasp on moralistic argument, and judged me to be unfit. You betrayed me, even when the truth was told. The fact is that transgender has nothing to do with a moral choice. It is an inborn and immutable physical reality!

As I went through my transition from what you made me be, to who I really am, you had "trouble with it." You felt so "confused." Oh really! Well, I was the one who suffered. I was the one who lost most of my life because of your wrong assignment. But you have "trouble with it!" If you had truly loved me, you would have rejoiced with me and adjusted. But you could not do that. You had to tell me that you were having trouble with "it," as though I was doing something wrong, when in fact, I was really making everything right!

I have struggled with my rage and my disillusionment over your stubbornness, until I realized that my anger would consume me. My rage would turn against me and strike out in suicide. But you would not learn from that. You would continue to betray others who, like me, struggle with the question "Who am I—boy or girl?" You would bury me with the gender name you imposed upon me when I was born-- the final cruel and eternal betrayal.

So I've decided that I will never commit suicide. I will channel the energy of my rage, and use it relentlessly, to help you grow to understand and accept me. My hope is that you will come to understand that my journey required a great deal of courage in the face of enormous difficulty. A journey that was filled with self doubt, the pain of loneliness, and your cruel reactive behavior, designed to force me to conform to the sex assignment you made upon me at birth, or suffer the consequences of emotional abuse, physical abuse, and the soul wrenching cruelty of generalized hatred and discrimination.

Now I am depleted of compassion over your having "trouble with it." My personal victory in rising above the catastrophe of a wrong sex assignment followed by a wrong gender socialization and enculturation, should earn for me your adulation and a sense of awe reserved for celebrities. I need more than just a smile and a shaky word of praise. I need applause, and all the trappings reserved for a hero. Then, I'll know that you are really serious in your acceptance of me. But perhaps you think I'm asking for too much. After all, other people suffer from social ignorance as well. Perhaps you'll feel that I'm asking for special treatment, like some pouting, angry, tear-filled adolescent.

But I have discovered that everything you did was wrong. That it was all backwards. I did not have a problem. I knew who I was. It was you who said I was a boy and expected me to be that way. I became the victim of Culturally Induced Stress Disorder (CISD). My stress and disillusionment was compounded by my feeling that in order to survive, I had no other alternative but to behave in the ways that you prescribed for me. My suffering the pain of anxiety, depression, guilt, shame, low self-esteem, and a sense of not belonging, was not my fault, but it was yours.

You said I suffered from the DSM IV diagnosis of Gender Identity Disorder. But all the while I knew who I was. I had no GID. You had GID all the time because you wouldn't accept the fact of my true sex identity, even after science supported me. When I came to psychotherapy, it was not to cure me from my need to be my true female self. It was to help me deal with the stresses of living in a world that refused to accept my true sex identity. Thank goodness there was a competent therapist who understood, who said I wasn't schizophrenic, nor was I suffering from dissociative personality disorder, nor did I need shock treatments that a transgendered friend of mine endured. After each shock treatment, she was asked if she still had thoughts of wanting to be a woman. When she said yes, they scheduled another shock treatment.

Now I see clearly. I see your betrayal. You are the fragile one. I hope you realize this too, and stop your fear-filled cruelty. Stop laughing at me. Stop rejecting me. Stop making me a scapegoat for your scorn. Stop "forgetting" to include me. Stop marginalizing me. Stop cultural systems from wounding me. Stop the sloppy health care and exclusions from health insurance coverage. Stop excluding me from anti-discrimination laws. Stop excluding me from meaningful work. Stop housing discrimination against me. Stop the coldness and rejection from churches or other spiritual communities that leave me feeling so hurt and so alone. Stop the generalized discrimination and hatred that makes my life so frighteningly uncertain.

Remember, I did not change my sex. I confirmed my real sex identity. I got it right after you made a wrong sex assignment followed by the wrong gender socialization and enculturation. I went through hell because you did not believe in me. You betrayed me…▼

Declaration
by Matthew Bartosik

I am gay.

For quite some time now.

Yes, I swish my hips
and I limp my wrist
pucker up my lips and blow

Such a cute pink triangle darling
Wherever did you get those shoes darling
Purple Power Darling

I'll stare that boy down
turn his head right 'round
make him bow to the ground
and make him cry out

Sissy   Pansy
  Fairy   Flamer
    Fruit   Fag
     Queer

I didn't know much about
queer sex growing up.

When I was seven
queer
Mom gave me a basic intro to "the birds and the bees"
and nothing else.

When I was thirteen
queer
a lady came to school to teach us all about our bodies and the
natural sex between a man and a woman
who are in love
and married of course.

When I was eighteen
queer
I couldn't explain why the natural, loving sex with my
girlfriend felt so queer?
strange.

And when I finally learned what the word meant,
I knew it was only said in two ways:
under hushed lips
queer
so no one would hear
or a loud proclamation of your humiliation
queer
in front of all who were near

And I'm supposed to be Proud to Be an American
Gazing upon the stars
knowing they don't want me in their army cars
Looking at the stripes
remembering how they beat us down with pipes
Saluting the flag for all it's worth
as they beat the fag right down to the earth
No

You want a patriot?
Well here I am
declaring War on your ass
bearing my flag in hand

The Rainbow Flag

Does this look like a sex flag to you?
It is my war flag.

See the red living blood we have shed for your sins
The orange sunsets where we restore our mental health
and a yellow sun that guides our way across
the green battlefields of your supposed "nature"
The blue tears we have cried in harmony
But most importantly the never-ending spirit that thrives
through our purple veins.

This is our rainbow.
This is our war.
This is the flag you will see as we tear down those straight
white picket fences that protect your ignorance
and set up those gender binaries

And as I come charging through your social constructs
I hold my flag with pride
letting out my war cry,

I am queer. ▼

*This submission is also available in poster format.
To purchase a poster please contact: The Collegiate EmPowerment Company
by calling toll free: 1-877-338-8246 or email: PosterInfo@Collegiate-EmPowerment.com.
Posters also be viewed and purchased online at: www.Collegiate-EmPowerment.com.
Thank you for your interest!

23 Ways to Put Trans Advocacy Into Action
by Lydia A. Sausa, M.S. Ed., Ph.D. candidate

"I felt alone and isolated. No one cared. No one really understood me and what I was going through. I loved school, but I never felt safe there because I was trans. I was threatened, followed, cornered, pushed, spit on, kicked, slapped, punched, beaten, and assaulted. I decided this is not the way I wanted to get an education and so I dropped out."- Keisha, age 21

Trans people transgress binary gender norms. They are a diverse population and are represented among every race, ethnicity, culture, socioeconomic class, and sexual orientation. Currently trans students, staff, and faculty face many challenges in colleges and universities due to discrimination, harassment, and violence. Schools are institutions of learning that stand for providing a safe educational and working environment for everyone, though we have failed in providing that for trans people on our campuses. As educators, students, advocates, and activists, it is time to step forward to first educate ourselves on the concerns and experiences of trans people, and then teach others in our schools what we have learned. To truly advocate for trans students and colleagues we must empower ourselves and others by identifying power imbalances, and creating opportunities to correct those power imbalances through collective action that transforms our educational institutions into safe and supportive environments.

I have known too many trans students who have been literally and figuratively beaten by ignorance and forced to drop out of school because of apathy. I have seen colleagues avoid wonderful careers in education or avoid coming out as trans, because they feared discrimination. Trans people are here. They are in our schools. They are the students in our classrooms. They are the staff and faculty members with whom we work with each day. They are our colleagues, our mentors, our friends. It is time to make some changes in our schools.

The following is a check list of ways to improve the educational and work environments of colleges and universities for trans students, staff, and faculty.

Update Policy and Forms:
1. Include gender expression and gender identity in your official university or college nondiscrimination policies. This helps to provide a safe educational and work environment for everyone, especially in matters of protecting against violence and harassment, and discrimination in tenure, promotion, student admissions, and financial aid.

2. Be gender inclusive with all forms, including surveys, administrative forms, applications. Do not limit gender and sex categories to "male" and "female," but also include "transgendered" or "trans" for students, staff, and faculty to check off. They may not always indicate they are trans or may check off more than one, but allow for possibilities. Another suggestion is simply to have the category say "gender identity," and then place a long dash after it for them to fill in.

3. Create specific guidelines about how to record, document, and address issues of harassment and verbal and physical abuse dealing with gender expression or gender identity, from student to student, employee to student, employee to employee, and student to employee.

4. Develop guidelines about how to assist trans students, staff, and faculty in navigating your school system, including

addressing concerns with bathrooms, locker rooms, residential living arrangements, school identification picture cards, name changes, requesting school transcripts after a name change, possible issues of harassment, etc.

Use Appropriate Language:

5. Provide workshops, guest speakers, and professional trainings to encourage students, staff, and faculty to use gender-neutral language and do not assume the sexual orientation of a trans person. For example, use parent or guardian instead of mother/father, use partner instead of girlfriend/boyfriend.

6. Respect trans people by using appropriate pronouns for their gender expression, or simply use their preferred name. When in doubt, ask! [Some people may prefer gender neutral pronouns such as "ze" instead of he or she, and "zir" instead of his or her.]

Create a Safe Environment:

7. Include trans literature, brochures, books, magazines, art work, and posters in your lobby or office. This helps people to feel welcomed and more comfortable.

8. Be an ally to and advocate for trans people. Create an atmosphere in which derogatory remarks regarding trans people are not acceptable. Challenge put-downs and dispel myths and stereotypes about the trans community.

9. Hire openly trans people as staff and faculty who would provide valuable knowledge about trans needs and concerns, as well as help trans students, and other trans staff and faculty feel represented in your college or university.

10. Encourage role models and mentors through special peer mentoring programs, and by having openly trans staff and faculty or trans allies who are trained and designated as "safe" peo-

ple to approach for information and support. This can be done for students as well as staff and faculty.

11. Establish support and discussion groups that are specific to addressing gender diversity and trans experiences.

12. Remove MEN'S and WOMEN'S restroom labels, or create additional gender inclusive restrooms. Many trans people have been harassed, even physically removed by security personnel, for entering the "wrong" bathroom. This is especially common for people who do not fit into the dichotomous gender norms of our society, such as a masculine or androgynous woman who has been mistaken as a "man" entering the WOMEN'S bathroom. To help create a safer atmosphere for trans students, staff, and faculty, universal gender inclusive RESTROOMS may be beneficial.

Increase Awareness & Provide Educational Training:

13. Take a trans sensitivity inventory of your college or university. Schedule periodic educational workshops and in-service trainings to provide important current information and assist with concerns or questions about the needs of trans people for your students, as well as your staff and faculty. Continual education is also helpful to address changes among staff and faculty, as well as the ever changing student body, and keep everyone up-to-date.

14. Ask for help from trans specific local and national organizations. Build collaborative relationships between your college and university and local centers, organizations, and support groups. If the resources at your college or university cannot meet the needs of a trans student, staff, or faculty member, put their best interests first, and refer them to someone who is better qualified or more experienced.

15. Hire specific point people to be trans resources for students, staff, and faculty. These people can be extremely advantages in assisting with concerns or questions, providing in-services or workshops for the school, and effectively dealing with everyday challenges in updating and representing a university or college on trans issues.

16. Have your campus Lesbian, Gay, Bisexual (LGB) Resource Center be inclusive of trans people as well. Please remember that simply adding the "T" at the end is not enough. Providing trans specific services, programs, resources, and creating a safe and welcoming space by a trained trans sensitive staff is essential for support, outreach, education, and advocacy. Encourage all LGB organizations, clubs, or school groups to be inclusive of trans people.

17. Encourage staff and faculty to include trans films, articles, books, guest speakers, and panels in their curricula to provide a place for open discussion, increased awareness, and education about the various issues affecting trans people.

18. Establish courses and encourage research which specifically address trans issues in the humanities, natural sciences, education, social sciences, and other disciplines.

19. Include information and training on trans youth issues in your college and university teacher education programs.

Establish Resources:

20. Designate resource people in your college or university to update and provide trans specific resources for students, staff, and faculty. These resources may include hotlines, listings of local and national trans organizations, listings of local support groups and medical providers who specifically service trans people, recent articles, books, and brochures. Having an accurate and current base of information is helpful for making effective referrals and attaining vital knowledge. Please make sure your personal or office libraries, as well as your college or university libraries, can provide current books and films on trans issues and experiences.

21. Fund students to attend trans specific conferences to educate themselves and encourage them to present their findings or share their information with campus organizations and others.

22. Be aware of the variety of current list serve discussion groups, web sites, and other electronic media for further information about trans people and their experiences. Also create special campus list serves as a way of providing support for students, staff, faculty and building connections to share.

23. Create a resource guide for trans students, staff, and faculty which include services, events, clubs and organizations on campus and in the local community that provide trans specific services and are trans friendly.

These are suggestions to begin implementing effective changes to improve the educational and work environments of our colleges and universities for trans students, staff, and faculty. Establish short and long term goals and work collaboratively with trans students, staff, and faculty toward achieving each of them. Though empowerment often begins with one person, it will affect countless numbers. ▼

Why I Do This
by James Hayes-Bohanan

I am a straight geography professor whose teaching and research specialties do not include queer studies. My reasons for becoming an active campus ally, therefore, do not relate directly to my personal identity or to my academic interests. I have become a visible ally for pedagogical reasons. That is, I think it makes me a better teacher.

I think the best college professors are those who educate the entire person. As important as the content of our disciplines may be, we can teach our students much more. Much of what I remember from my own college professors are life lessons that were not in the curriculum.

I advocate for GLBT students and staff, but I think the primary beneficiaries are my straight students. I believe my advocacy helps to prepare them as citizens and future professionals. My straight colleagues benefit for similar reasons.

One simple encounter helped me to realize, however, my activism can help me to be a better teacher for GLBT students. One day a few years ago "Sarah" came to my office at that time of the semester – just after half-way – that students often come by. It began as a fairly typical visit with an introductory student who has just realized that she has fallen behind and needs to redouble her efforts in order to succeed in the class. She chided herself for not working harder, and asked about what she needed to do for the rest of the semester.

Then, something changed. She burst into tears and said, "eye-jeskeemowtomeyemdr!"

"What?" I asked, and was glad I keep tissues on the desk.

"I just came out to my mother."

This student knew I was an ally, and I had already seen her at campus events where she was out. I did not turn this into a counseling session about her coming out to her family, but I could see in an instant that being able to tell just one professor what was really going gave her a great sense of relief. She did not use it as an excuse, but naming the problem enabled her to move on. She got caught up in her work, and completed the course successfully. Several semesters later, when it was time to graduate, Sarah honored me with an invitation to attend the President's Toast with her. This is a special program for graduating seniors, and Sarah is the only student who has invited me as her guest.

My experience with Sarah was rewarding on a personal level, but it also shows that advocacy for GLBT students can contribute to their academic success. By having a safe place to release some of her emotions surrounding her coming-out process, Sarah was able to refocus her energies during that difficult semester. ▼

Just Another Guy
by Brian Coyle

Joe's college life was filled with homework, classes, working to pay expenses, and partying with his fraternity brothers. He never felt so accepted and included as he did since pledging. Joe's roommate at the fraternity house, Chris, was an okay guy who was a football player, dating a sorority president, and although sometimes obnoxious, he was usually fun to hang out with. One night Joe came home late from his job at a local restaurant to find his half of the room in shambles.

"What the hell is this, Joe?" Chris asked angrily as he waved something in Joe's face.

Joe's heart almost stopped when he realized what it was. They were magazines of naked men that Joe had kept in an envelope, buried at the bottom of his trunk. Joe knew he had not left them out in plain sight and now hated himself for buying them.

Joe's hands trembled; his legs were like jelly as he took a step towards Chris. "Look, man let's talk about this."

"Back off, faggot!" Chris yelled. "Don't you ever come near me again. Get out of my room, now! I'm not sleeping in this room with you dreaming about me. Get out!" Chris yelled again as he shoved Joe against the wall. "Get out or you'll wish you had."

Joe just sat on the front steps of the fraternity house, fighting back tears. "Maybe I should just kill myself," Joe thought out loud. This idea was no stranger to Joe's mind as he always felt like his life was a useless lie anyway. But now the truth was creeping out and it was neither freeing or a relief, it was terrifying.

Headlights smacked Joe out of his daze as a car pulled up to him.

"Hey Joe, what are you doing out here?" David asked.

"Um, I locked myself out of my room. It's late so I didn't know where to go."

Joe needed someone to talk to and wanted to trust somebody but he couldn't tell David the truth. David always seemed like a good guy with a level head, liberal attitude, and sense of fairness, but he was president of the fraternity, a football player, Homecoming King, and Chris' best friend.

"You sure that's it? You look really terrible."

"I'm just going through some stuff right now. You wouldn't understand, nobody would."

"How do you know if you don't talk about it?" David queried. "Follow me to my apartment and you can crash there."

Joe hesitated but then agreed. The next day, Joe crept out early from his night on David's couch and although he tried to avoid his fraternity brothers all day, he did run into a few, but they acted normal towards him.

After an agonizing debate, Joe dragged himself to the fraternity meeting that night. He was the treasurer and needed to give his report. He also wanted to talk to Chris before the meeting and straighten things out but he arrived at the house late. Waves of noise and laughter filled the room as he approached it, but complete silence fell on the group as Joe shut the door behind him and made his way to the officer's table at the front.

All eyes were on him and there was snickering in every row as he passed. "There's a motion on the floor to have your pin pulled and expel you from the fraternity," We aren't going to let some homo ruin our reputation and make us the campus joke.

As soon as David gets here, we can make it official," Chris beamed with pride.

Joe just sat in silence, unable to move, and glared out at the sea of faces that he thought were his friends, his brothers. Joe finally decided to leave. He would just quit and transfer schools if he had to. He gathered the strength to stand up and walked quickly to the door, opened it, and ran right into David.

"What the hell is going on in here?" David yelled, annoyed.

"We're just about to black ball Joe but need you to officiate," Chris smiled.

"What are you talking about?" David raised his voice at Chris.

"What are they talking about," he asked again, softly, directly to Joe.

"I'm sorry, Dave" was all Joe could say as tears filled his eyes and he pushed past him and ran out the front door.

The next day, David caught up with Joe outside of English class. Joe's weary eyes betrayed him when he said that he hadn't been up all night worrying.

"I'm so sorry you had to go through that, Joe"

"You are?"

"Those guys are jerks and they had no right to humiliate you like that. Chris had no right to go through your stuff either. Here, take this," David said and handed him a key.

"What's this?" Joe asked, confused.

"You are going to stay with me for a while." Joe was finally able to lift his head from his shame and look at David as he continued, "We had a very long meeting last night and talked things out. It is going to take a while for some of the guys, but most of them don't care if you're gay or not."

"I never said I was gay!"

"Whatever the case, Chris shouldn't have set off this chain of events and made judgments about you. He's a big mouth. I can't guarantee that what happened won't get around, but I asked that the guys let you figure things out for yourself."

"They will always be talking behind my back. What makes you think that these guys are going to let me back in?"

"Because they like you, and they like me."

"What are you talking about, Dave?"

"I came out at last night's meeting Joe."

"Wwwwhat?"

"The reason I was coming by late that night was because I had been on a date with a guy. I couldn't be silent any longer."

"I don't know what to say, Dave. You have saved my life, literally. You don't know how desperate I was. I always wished that there was just another guy out there like me that would understand."

"I want you to know that you always have someone to talk to. I'm here. There are professionals right here on campus who are here to listen. There is no shame in asking for help.

You aren't the only one going through this so don't feel alone. We are in this together now, Joe. Why don't we stop by the house and shoot some hoops with the guys and then head home and talk about it," David smiled. ▼

The Inspiration Book Series

Sumthin
by Sabrina Santa Clara

She used to get a kind of
crazy look in her eyes when I dolled up with
burgundy lipstick, chunky black boots
pants riding low around the hips of my bare skin
with a cross round the ring on the lip of my navel
pointing like a neon sign straight down towards my
pantiless pussy

there was a clear switch
when love and appreciation turned into
the creepy ogling of my grandfather
or los vatos que me llamaban
that would cruise by me slowly
playing the oldies loud in their low riders
that jerked low and high like some kind of weird
mechanical fuck machine

She never understood why I'd pull away then
after spending an hour or more to get the perfect San
Francisco fem-butch don't you wanna fuck me look

And I couldn't figure out how
after waiting 30 damn years to love a woman
I was
One More Fucking Time,
relegated to the back seat like some cheap ass

Southern Californian
love me from the outside chick 'cause their ain't
nothing going on inside
this head
this heart
this hollow called a soul

I didn't understand then
how I gave her the same power I had given
All Those Men
and made less of myself so that she would
love me
want me
make me feel like I had purpose for being
because of what lay between my legs.

And now,
skirting round the edges of 37
I know the Difference between loving
a man
and a woman
ain't nothing until
I
make in sumthin ▼

The Strength of Friendship
by Thomas A. Feldman

Ironically, it was at one of the most heterosexual events that this could have happen....a wedding. My good friend Rich was about to watch his sister take the plunge into married bliss. I ran around my room trying to look presentable for the evening and thinking of how much fun I was going to have that night, having NO idea this night would also be an inspirational turning point in my life.

Now, let me flashback to about three month earlier. I had been dealing with my sexuality, but had come out to a VERY select group. Even those whom I was closest to, including my best friends, were still in the dark, or so I thought.

I would be graduating from college with honors soon. One evening, after deciding to treat myself to a celebratory "night out," I drove to a local gay bar with plenty of room to dance and have fun. It never bothered me to go out on my own once and a while. To me, it was therapeutic and allowed me to just dance and do my thing until I looked like a reject from a Richard Simmons workout video (at which time I knew is was time to go home).

I planned this night in July to be like many others, where I would go, dance, and go home. I was not looking for a date. And when I was too pooped to "get giggy with it" anymore, the bar had a patio out back that allowed me to just sit out, relax and people watch underneath the gorgeous night sky. And although I did enjoy coming to this place, I felt my time there was getting a little stale.

As I looked around the patio, I saw many individuals who fit the gay stereotype. A life of club hopping from weekend to weekend was not the kind of life I wanted. I sat there and said to myself, "Is this all there is?" If by me coming out meant that my life would be club hopping every weekend until I became that guy that you make fun of at the bar, I was not interested. You know who I am talking about, the guy who looks as if he should have left that party two years ago. I realize this sounds ridiculous to have been thinking that deeply at that moment, but I was. Staying in the closet and marrying some poor girl to just save my life from a world of dance clubs is laughable, but I also was aware I needed more than this. I had never felt so lost in all my 24 years on this planet. After pondering this thought for a few more minutes and realizing I was slipping into my own, overly dramatic soap opera, I took a few more sips of my beer and I said to myself, "Enough already! Lighten up! It's late and it's time to get back on that dance floor for one last song and then it's time to head home."

The dance floor was on two levels, one of which was elevated three feet higher than the majority of the rest of the floor. I hopped up on the elevated part and joined the other patrons in dancing to Madonna's "Human Nature" (tell me God doesn't have a sense of humor) and then the lightning bolt hit. Out of the corner of my eye was this unknown face that I felt as if I had known it forever. Stunning myself, since I rarely ever went up and introduced myself to anyone first, I jumped off the platform and made a beeline to this unknown, familiar soul. After trying to scream my name over the music and misunderstanding his because of the blaring dance beats, we decided to go out on the patio and talk. We talked for over an hour about so many subjects and I was finding myself enthralled by whatever he said. As the bar was preparing to kick everyone out for the evening, I walked him to his car, where he gave me his number. "I am staying with my aunt and uncle for the summer before I leave for school, and I want you to call me." At that point I responded with some lame compliment that everyone seems to say when they are excited and clueless at the same time. This was not just a silly crush or someone to just brag about over the next few days. As odd as it may sound, but as soon as he drove away, I knew my life would never be the same.

My newly found soul mate was planning to attend graduate school in Indiana, which meant he would be leaving for the Hoosier state in a few short weeks. Those weeks we had before he left were wonderful. He was intelligent and wanted to make a difference in the world. He was kind and funny and I never wanted to let him go. More and more, instead of happy though, I was becoming increasingly frustrated to the point where I just wanted him to go. Why, because I knew when he went off to school, he would have a new life and there would be little room for someone like me who was over two hundred miles away. I was starting to fall for him hard, in a way I didn't believe was possible for two men. It scared me. The day before he left for school was one of the most wonderful and sad days of my life.

After he was at school, I drove down for a few weekends, and although we had a wonderful time, he was wrapped up, and rightfully so, in his graduate studies. New friends, new faces and I was becoming a summer footnote.

At the end of September was the wedding of my friend's sister. As the evening drew to a close and the band was playing the tired music that is a staple at any wedding, I sat at the head table of the reception by myself, drinking way too many glasses of wine and becoming more and more upset. Why couldn't he be here to enjoy this with me? Why am I scared to tell these wonderful people around me who I really was? At that moment, my best friend's girlfriend grabbed me by the arm and dragged me out into the parking lot of the wedding hall. I had no clue what was going on, but I was sober enough to realize this wasn't just happening in my head. Lisa stopped me in the middle of the parking lot and just looked me in the eyes. That is all she had to do was look me in the eyes. I began sobbing hestarically (I mean LIFETIME; Television for WOMEN sobbing) and told I her I was gay. Now Lisa is an incredibly beautiful women in the first place. But seeing the compassion in her face made her all the more radiant. I even stopped mid-sentence to apologize for getting tears and snot all over her purple evening dress. We both laughed. A minute later, Lisa turned from laughter into the stern educator she was studying to become and said, "We know what you are going through, Tom, but why won't you let us help you?" "Danny and I, as well as everyone else love you for who you are and we are worried about you." She continued on, stating that none of them could understand why I was saying NOTHING.

It felt as if we were in the parking lot for hours. It was surreal. But as it turned out, that was just the beginning of my "coming out" night. I have to give my friends credit for their excellent organizational skills, because as soon as Lisa and I were done talking, I was whisked away in a car by my extraordinary friend Rich. I felt like Ebenizer Scrooge without the money or snow. Where as Lisa was "The ghost of Straight Past," Rich was "The Ghost of Gay Present." We drove all over town, talking in the car, stopping at local pubs for a drink and more talking. I told Rich everything. I told him about "my soulmate." I told him about the guilt I was feeling. I talked, I screamed, I cried and he listened. Rich is an incredible listener and has a knack for making anyone realize what an idiot they are being without being overly critical or mean. "Don't you see how bottling all this emotion up inside is driving you nuts?!" He then went on, "...and if this 'soulmate' doesn't realize how special YOU are, then he isn't worth your time!" It had to be almost 4 o' clock in the morning before he finally dropped me off. If I loved my friends before, I adored them now.

And again, realizing what a wonderful sense of humor God must have in even the most insane of situations, one of the bridesmaids needed a ride home and was in the back seat of Rich's car. I think we both forgot about her and she came everywhere we went that night. To this day, I think that girl is scared of me.

With a new found confidence, knowing that my friends were behind me 100%, I came out and I have never regretted it for one minute. Their strength has given me the courage to handle adversity and has given me the confidence to know I AM on the right path. I have never looked back.

Oh, as for "The Ghost of Gay Future," everything worked out with my soulmate and we have been together now for seven years. ▼

Within A Cage Of Your Own
by Raul Medina

Living La Vida Medea
by Reid Vanderburgh, MA

I was 39-years-old, living as a lesbian, when I first realized I'd probably be happier living as a guy. I did not take kindly to this realization, for several reasons. First, I had quite a life built up in the Portland (Oregon) lesbian community. I was a founding member of nine years' standing of the Portland Lesbian Choir, and leaving that group was not on my horizon.

Second, I had a family of choice with whom my bonds were stronger than those with my biological family. All were lesbians. All were fellow Choir members, or members of my mixed chorus, Bridges Vocal Ensemble. Or members of both. Queer folks find family as we are able, and often the bonds forged through living in a hostile society are stronger than the bonds of blood connection. I was scared of my realization – if I became a man, would I lose my family of choice?

Finally, I had a negative reaction to the idea of being trans because I had absorbed the mainstream belief that being trans was weird, sick and perverted. I had some vague equation of "transsexual" and "drag queen" as synonymous, which of course had made it impossible for me to recognize myself as a transsexual earlier in my life. I've loathed feminine clothing for as long as I can remember, which is hardly the attitude of a drag queen!

I'd never had conscious fantasies about being male. I had just never felt completely at home in my skin as a female, causing a low-grade anxiety and depression that was growing steadily as I aged. I hated women's bathrooms. I did not like introducing myself to others, as my former name was highly feminine. I avoided describing myself as a lesbian, and felt vaguely uncomfortable referring to myself as a woman. I had never visited an ob/gyn in my life. I was full of contradictions and felt an enigma to myself – not an easy life for a Virgo.

I would probably still be living in denial had my then-partner not come out to me in the spring of 1995, telling me one night, "I've always felt like a man inside." This effectively held a mirror to my soul. I could no longer ignore what I saw there, but was not prepared to face it. The effect was rather like a badly-done substance abuse intervention. Because of the negative attitudes I'd internalized about what it meant to be trans.

Then one day a bisexual friend said to me, with some envy in her voice, "What a gift, to be able to live as both sexes in one lifetime." This one phrase reframed the experience for me, for the first time putting a positive spin on the concept of being trans. Nowhere else had I encountered a positive interpretation of what it might mean to be trans. I moved forward with great confidence and excitement at the possibilities inherent in the unexpected opportunity life had presented me.

I postponed my physical transition for nearly two years, waiting for the Portland Lesbian Choir to record its first CD. I spent those two years in gender limbo-land, being seen primarily as male in my undergrad classes at Portland State University (unless I opened my mouth to speak), being seen as in transition at work, and being seen as a lesbian during Choir rehearsals. I felt the split keenly, never being able to quite integrate these various aspects of my life into one cohesive whole, despite the fact that I came out to everyone who was important to me. Transition cannot be done in the closet.

Once I began hormones and had top surgery, life became much simpler, as my former lesbian life faded away gradually. However, what I found is that I did not become more male in my outlook on life. I became fully male in appearance, while retaining many of the values I'd learned in the lesbian community. I did not feel much more comfortable calling myself a man than I had calling myself a woman, or a lesbian, though I felt fine calling myself a guy and definitely felt more comfortable in my own skin. I did not lose my lesbian family of choice, and found those friendships have retained their original intimacy. If anything, they are deeper than ever, as I am more centered and thus more capable of truly intimate relationships.

I gradually came to realize I had not transitioned from female to male. I had transitioned from female to not female. In the ensuing years, I have come to agree with Kate Bornstein, a transwoman writer and performer, who stated in her book Gender Outlaw, "I know I'm not a man – about that much I'm very clear, and I've come to the conclusion that I'm probably not a woman, either."

I wasn't raised to be a man. I did not absorb male socialization. I did not have testosterone dominant in my body, with the resulting imperious sex drive, until I was 41-years-old. I have never thought of women as other than my equal, and don't believe I can.

I've become increasingly convinced, both through personal experience and through conversations with other trans people, that it's not really possible to transition fully from one sex to another. Many assume this must mean I'm gay (I don't identify as such), as the thought never enters their minds that perhaps I wasn't always male. Those biomen who know I'm trans sometimes utilize me as a resource for understanding women's ways of seeing the world, though I have always been treated respectfully by these men.

Biowomen see me as a man, though they quickly come to realize there's something not quite man-like about me. Women, however, tend to feel completely comfortable with me in a way many biomen do not – they subconsciously recognize me as "one of them," though not in a way that makes me feel uncomfortable. It does not feel as if they are seeing me as a woman.

I feel I'm neither man nor woman, though the limitations of English force me to choose sides, if only so I may have terminology with which to describe myself. So, I'm a guy, much more comfortable with male pronouns than female, but not really feeling like "a man." I'm living la vida medea – life in the middle. I have not crossed the bridge from "female" on one side, over an immeasurable chasm, to become "male" on the other side. Rather, I have become the bridge. ▼

Gay Pride On Parade
by Shane L. Windmeyer

red, orange, yellow, green, blue, purple flying high
dykes on bikes, pflag moms, flaming firemen, screaming queens
gay pride on parade

hot summer heat, pink sequence, corporate logos everywhere
amazon girls, hrc equality, silver muscle boys rocking on
gay pride on parade

warm embrace, holding hands, gay moms,
gay dads with kids shouting 'we are family'
band marches on, water guns squirting,
hate-filled bigots protesting who we are
gay pride on parade

doctors, lawyers, shaved hard pecs shirtless hunks,
frat boy letters standing proud
rainbow floats, police on patrol keeping check,
women's rugby playing hard
gay pride on parade

gays for jesus, leather daddy,
lesbians shooting bras free up up away
gender express and identity, people to love,
safer sex to stop HIV
gay pride on parade

pink m&ms, lots of lube, dental dams,
rainbow boas flapping in air
atheists, out loud teachers in the classroom,
lipstick lesbians looking fine
gay pride on parade

log cabin republican, stonewall democrat,
get out the rainbow vote in November
gay, lesbian, bi, fem boy, butch boy, trans, we are all proud
gay pride on parade

multi-color faces in a crowd, smiles wide across the streets
floats redecorate, people change, a spectrum of our diversity
gay pride on parade

red, orange, yellow, green, blue, purple flying high
that's a part of me, march on and celebrate, my community
gay pride on parade ▼

The Inspiration Book Series

Here Today, Gone Tomorrow
by Lizzy Conley

I've lost my rainbow necklace. I must mourn its passing. I bought it just last month at Pride, my first Pride ever. Actually, though, the last Pride I was still relatively closeted. I believe it was around the time that I came out to my mother. Around the time that I lost count of those people at school who knew (I got to something like forty-five before I realized that not only had I lost track, but I didn't really care to be careful anymore). Around the time that I probably really would have enjoyed Pride, but been too uncomfortable to really take advantage of it.

So this year I went with three other queer-ies from school, and I bought myself a necklace. It had tan wooden beads most of the way around, but in the front there was a rainbow bit about three inches long. I was so proud of myself. I used to be cautious about wearing rainbow, lest someone think I was gay and not bi. I wanted to show pride in my sexuality, but I didn't want to give any members of the opposite sex the wrong idea. The closest I could find was a button, "Of course, SOME people DO go BOTH ways". But that took explaining, and most people don't take the time to read one button among many. I was out, but not Out.

It wasn't until recently that I said to hell with worrying about what people will think, let them get to know me. Not to mention the fact that I'm pretty much out to any and all who'd care now. You think I'm a lesbian? Okay, you're 2/3 right. Straight? Sure, some of the time. Bi? Yeah, you could call me that, although I'm finding all three labels too confining as of late.

Because what are these labels, anyway? At first I took pleasure in being able to proclaim my bisexuality, but now not only does it sound too… well… straight for me, but it's so… common. I know that one shouldn't define oneself by how one feels about a label's reputation, but let's face it, bisexuality's got a bad rap. I'd rather just be queer and be done with it.

So here I was, proudly wearing my rainbow necklace. I'd taken a cue from a Californian lesbian jazz pianist /punk rocker that I'd met over the summer at a music program and saw how much easier it could make things. Sure, coming out to large groups of people that you don't know very well can be fun at times, but it's much easier to give them a little hint of color before blindsiding them with a choice piece of information. Yes, I do like girls. I lot. Butch ones, femme ones, feminist ones, model ones, you show me a girl and I'm pretty likely to admire something about her. You got a problem wit' that?

The thing was, I was no longer in large groups of people who would be surprised by such knowledge. I was just going to school like always, reminding people of something that they all certainly knew by now. Still, it was comforting to have this tangible symbol of my gaiety. Here I am world, quite queer.

And then suddenly my symbol was gone. I'd actually been volunteering at a local thrift store that benefits glbt causes, and driving home in the car I suddenly felt my neck and there was nothing there. Was this a sign? Did I no longer need to wear my sexuality as though it were a race? Nah. I don't think so. That's why I'm going to be getting another one real quick. I may be out, but if one closeted stranger sees me on the street and finds some comfort in my ability to be open, I'll be satisfied. ▼

Not An Average Day
by Wanda L.E. Viento

It was late and I was tired. These 14-hour days were getting to be too much for me. As a full-time doctoral student *and* coordinator of Lesbian, Bisexual, and Gay Student Services at Western Michigan University, I had little time in my life for anything else. After a long, busy day, I just wanted to go home and go to sleep. I still had one more stop to make after the LBGTA student group meeting.

It was September and the presidential race was in full swing. George W. Bush was to speak at a small, homophobic Christian college in the area and students wanted to make signs for their protest. I need to unlock the office for them, and then I was going home to bed. I drove up to the building and parked in a no-parking zone. I would only be one minute and didn't want to hike the several blocks from a legitimate parking space.

As I approached the building, it was dark but I could see a group of students were already waiting for me under the light of the building. Their energy was high and giddy, their activism new and exciting for them. I smile, feeling a rush. I do love this job.

They greeted me with cheers and taunts as I unlocked the door and welcomed them to use whatever they could find in my office. After a stampeding rush of bodies went up the stairs, one student remained behind. Matt was a first-year who showed up in my office the very first week of school. Like many of the students coming to Western, he was from a small, rural town. Being in a "big city" like Kalamazoo can be overwhelming. I often hear how exciting it is for students to finally meet other LBGT folk, and a lot of first year students go a little berserk in the beginning with their newfound freedom and alliances.

Matt was chewing his nails anxiously.

"Wanda, I gotta talk to you."

I was so tired. This was probably one more relationship crisis.

"Matt, can it wait till tomorrow?"

"No, no it can't. It's really important! I gotta talk to you tonight. Please."

My stomach lurched. My sleepiness dissipated. I've had to deal with relationship issues, grades, coming out to parents, being disowned by family, losing financial aid, harassment on and off campus, but I've never had to hear a student tell me he was HIV positive. I think that's my biggest fear. I started to catch his anxiety.

"Ok, Matt. Let me go move my car."

I parked my car and on the walk back to the building, I worked to keep myself calm. When I got back to Ellsworth Hall, Matt was pacing outside still chewing on his nails and smoking a cigarette. I saw him put out his cigarette when I approached and appreciated the gesture. The students know I don't like being around smoke and have shown a good deal of respect for that.

"Ok. Do you want to go inside?"

"No, let's stay out here. I don't want any of them to hear."

The night was a little nippy, but Michigan was still experiencing the last dregs of summer. We walked over to a nearby bench and sat.

"Well, what's going on?"

"Wanda, I don't know what to do! Oh God, I really don't know what to do!"

I tried to remain calm at the urgency in his voice. I was trying to guess what else it might be other than my fear.

"About what, Matt?"

"Oh God. Wanda, I think… Oh God!"

At this point, tears were coming down his face. I ached for him.

"Wanda, I think… I think I might be straight." His shaking hands covered his face at that point.

Did I hear right? For a moment, I had a strange, surreal sensation. The lapse in time was immeasurable at this point.

"You what?"

"I think I might be straight. Oh God, what am I going to do? My parents will kill me! After everything I've put them through. My parent will kill me if they find out I'm straight!"

I really wasn't very clear on what to say or do. None of my classes ever trained me for this scenario!

"Ok, first of all Matt, take a couple of deep breaths and let's slow down."

Was I saying this for him or for me? Either way, he did take some breaths, which gave me a couple of seconds to collect my thoughts.

"What has happened to make you think you might be heterosexual?"

"Well, there's this girl…"

(Ugh! Most of my students know my aversion to the word 'girl,' but now was not the time to correct sexism.)

"…on my floor. She's really nice and she reminds me of my best friend back home. I like talking to her and doing stuff with her. I just like being with her I guess."

"How is this different from your other female friends?"

"Well, I don't know. I feel attracted to her I think."

"Attracted how, Matt?"

"Ummm, I don't know".

"Sexually?"

"I don't think so. I just like being with her a lot."

"Ok. Well, how do you feel about Jason? And Dustin? And Taylor?" These were all guys he had had crushes on so far this year.

"Oh, shit, they're so hot!"

"So you haven't stop being attracted to men?"

"God, no, Wanda!"

"How about other women around here? Any other attractions?"

"No, no, no…." He was slowing down, finally, still gnawing on his cuticles though.

"So you're still attracted to men—a lot; you're attracted to one woman, but not sexually."

"When you put it that way…"

"Look, Matt, you came out when you were 14. Now you're 18. It's possible that you're just now beginning to see all the aspects of who you are. You know, some theories of sexuality place us on a continuum, not in categories. I think we all have aspects of attraction to men and to women to some degree. It's a matter of where we fall on that continuum."

"You don't think I'm turning straight?"

"Well, anything's possible! But, no, I don't think you're 'turning straight.' I think you're discovering other aspects of who you are."

"God, I'm so relieved! I don't have to tell my parents I'm straight! Thank you, Wanda! Thank you!" He finally stopped gnawing his nails long enough to give me a hug.

"OK?"

"OK. I'm going to go make signs now. See you tomorrow."

"OK."

In fact, I did see Matt the next day. He was back to his usual self. But me?

I got a little less sleep. And, I had had one of the strangest conversations in my tenure as coordinator—kids freaking about being straight. Who knows what the world will bring tomorrow. ▼

Flamer
by Mike Esposito

Hush, Hush
by Rhianne Paz Bergado

Hush hush keep it down now
voices carry it's not that I'm ashamed of you
But I have cause to be wary, instinctively thoughts roll off my tongue
Don't you know two rights only make one wrong
You're just young and mistaken, Leviticus Abomination
You don't know any better then to face the degradation
Just take the cash settlement, less hassle then a trial
Just walk this Kilometer sounds shorter then a mile,
It must be so hard not to know who you are
But we know what better to do with you by far
After all we invented it along with the Internet,
Along with Missionaries and colonization for the sinners and
Everytime I turn around you're on that Jerry Springer show
Sleepin' with your sister and pimpin somebody's ho, man,
sometimes you people make me sick
And I think you belong in Wyoming on a fence post crucifix
You should just stay in the closet
and everything that could possibly cause it
I've set out to destroy
Words of hatred I deploy in my rap lyrics
and don't act like you don't hear it
when I say "That's Gay"
it's to remind you everyday
that you're wrong and I'm right
despite your struggles and your strife
I'm gonna be here laugh at you

cause I'm leading a normal life
I dare you implore you inform you
There is a resistance ready to conform you
and I dare you to show me
what you find true in this world
and I dare you to show me
are you a boy or are you a girl
and I dare you once more to justify
hate in the name of God
injustice in the name of Allah
and Bigotry written into our laws
and I dare you once more
what have you found true in this world
this world that hates and fears me
When I'm just another girl.

Hush, hush, keep it down now
voices carry, it's not that I'm ashamed of you.

Hush, hush, keep it down now
voices carry, it's not that I'm ashamed of you.

Hush, hush, keep it down now
voices carry, it's not that I'm ashamed of you. ▼

*This submission is also available in poster format.
To purchase a poster please contact:
The Collegiate EmPowerment Company by calling toll free: 1-877-338-8246
or email: PosterInfo@Collegiate-EmPowerment.com. Posters also be viewed
and purchased online at: www.Collegiate-EmPowerment.com.
Thank you for your interest!

A Pioneering Tradition
by Greg Darnell

In the fall, I entered the community of Transylvania University in Lexington, Kentucky full of excitement and eagerness to learn, grow, and be on my own in the collegiate atmosphere. The campus was small with a little more than 1,000 students but full of Greek life and tradition dating as far back as the first decade of the 19th century. I had heard much about the Greek community of Transy from alumni in my hometown and was already being rushed heavily before I even enrolled for classes. From this and ever since I had visited campus as a high school senior, I looked forward to joining a Greek organization. Though my parents seemed staunchly against it, I did not heed their advice.

When rush approached the third week of the first academic semester, I was ready to show these guys who I was, well at least a little of who I was, and show the alumni my eagerness to be one of them. I was ready to join a fraternity, a membership, as I was told, of like-minded men who loved each other, took care of one another, and had great times living college life to its fullest. A grand idea for a small-framed closeted homosexual like myself, being one of those high school boys that always had a propensity to never have a girlfriend, hang out with females much of the time, and get uncomfortable in the locker room.

I rushed that fall, eager but very apprehensive about trusting these older guys with my loyalty. I feared they would turn upon me if they knew my secret and might even say things like "You're a fag?, What the hell are you doing in here?, Don't try to hit on me." Etc.

Despite these fears, I pledged Delta Sigma Phi and strove to be a valiant pledge. The program breezed by, much to my surprise, and I had a good time getting to know my other pledge brothers and learning about what the fraternity was going to offer me. Soon thereafter, I received my activation notice, was elected service chairman, and went through all the motions of being a good "straight" active.

Even after I was initiated and had the pressure of getting in relieved, I still kept my life a secret, so much so that my fellow brothers knew little about me aside from the classroom. I tried intently to keep all suspicions away from my love life and preference. I always took a friend (girl) to a function, and I never talked about dating, always coming up with the excuse that I was too busy for such things.

Becoming super involved on campus to show others my worth was a main way to cope, because deep inside I felt full of the sin my parents and church had always correlated with homosexual people. I never talked to any of the loud, "flaming" gay people on campus, fearing that even the slightest interaction might send people spreading rumors. I avoided the gay unity group during the organizational fairs and never voiced my opinion in class about gay relationships, marriage, and rights. Sadly, I was your typical closeted fraternity member, and I was unhappy as ever, though I portrayed the exact opposite night and day.

Sophomore year came and went; I received more fraternity appointments/offices, lived with many of my brothers on our fraternity hall, was named sweetheart of a campus sorority, and consequently tried harder to hide myself. That year, I found the wonders of the Internet in forming correspondences with other closeted boys such as myself. Dating was a thing only done at night, far away from campus where no one would see. I remember vividly leaving my dorm at 1:00 a.m. to go and have coffee with my boyfriend driving around Lexington just to be alone with him, all the time scared that someone might see me in a restaurant alone with a guy. I look back now and realize how much paranoia can set in when you hide so much of yourself and look to no one for help. I couldn't even reach out to my best friends at the time, because I feared that even they would leave me.

In my junior year, I realized I was the unhappiest person both with myself and with other people. I had the propensity to snap out at my friends, become defensive under the most non-threatening situations, and be obsessive about things that did not matter. I never had fun at functions anymore, and I didn't like hanging around some of the guys because of their derogatory comments muttered in front of me and in meeting. When this was all coming to a head, I wanted to deactivate and get the hell out of the oppressive atmosphere I was living in.

Then one event spurred me to reevaluate both my position and my potential to change my environment. In meeting one night, I found out through talking with brothers that our alumni corporation board president was an out gay man and very comfortable with himself. This piqued my interest, and after much thought, I decided to ask this guy to dinner and tell him my situation. We went to dinner, I apprehensively told him I was gay, and through the conversation, I found out much about gay fraternity life in general and really how many of us there are in the community. It was a staggering realization: "Gay people do exist in fraternities. There are a lot of them. I can be one too." Our alumni president told me stories of his times at Transy, his hardships and how he handled it all back in his day. These stories showed me a new path that appealed to what I wanted to accomplish. I wanted to be in a fraternity that fostered tolerance, love, loyalty, and actual brotherhood, which so many chapters boast about. I wanted to be able to be myself at functions, talk to whomever I wanted whenever I wanted, and have a boyfriend without being ashamed. And from then on, I set out to do it.

At first, the process was slow. I pulled my closest brothers aside one on one and confided in them, marking their reactions and seeing what problems they had. To my astonishment, they all accepted me as they would have if I were straight. They understood my frustration with myself and the fraternity, and most actually encouraged me to change the perception of gay people in fraternity life. They loved me no less than they did before and were really proud that I had the courage to tell them. The sisters of the sorority met me with open arms and loving advice on how to better my situation and get my brothers to see me for who I really was.

By the end of my junior year, I had let my guard down considerably. I talked to many of the guys in my fraternity about me being gay and brought up issues with them about respect, comments, and other things that were offensive to someone such as myself. I took my boyfriend to two formals that year, at which events we did dance together and were a couple just as the other straight couples were all around us. That was probably the biggest step for me to have taken with my brotherhood. I wanted them to not only accept the idea of being gay and a brother but also see a gay brother being just that. Additionally, I tried to better the stereotype many brothers had about gay men and gay brothers. It took a lot of work to answer the questions they had, allay their worries, and encourage their honesty with me, but it was well worth the effort. The functions, the conversations, and the parties all were positive testimonies to the power of honesty and brotherhood.

As I stand on the verge of graduation and reminisce on my past here at Transylvania, I see that my biggest accomplishment was finally accepting who I was, what I do in my life, and how to at least be comfortable with others. It was a rough and winding road, but I have never been happier in my life as I am now within my fraternity. I am completely out on campus and look forward to the times I have left here. I bring gay guys to functions at times, hang out with gay friends in the presence of my brothers, and talk gay issues both at meeting and behind closed doors with brothers.

Though my situation now seems nothing but positive, there were times during this journey when I felt completely alone and without anyone to understand. I wanted to leave it all behind and be bitter and jaded at the social injustices of it all. But my conscience would not let me leave in that manner. I had to change my situation, let others understand the misconceptions, and know that brotherhood can exist in this way. I had faith in myself, my fraternity, and its time-honored ideals.

Truly, I have been fortunate enough to find within the ritual bonds of brotherhood the true meaning of fraternity. I feel the friendships that fraternities should foster; I experience the chance to be at a social gathering with someone I care for. I understand what respect and honesty means to those who practice it, and above all I learned how to live a life proudly, knowing that one person can make a difference by being himself. For some people out there, this experience is opposite than of their own. For those individuals, I extend my condolences, but as for me, I can say that the work I have put in to helping my situation is something I will never forget and something of which I will always be proud. ▼

Rainbow Flag Seven
by Ken Schneck

I was never an activist.

I'm gay. I date men. End of story.

Junior year of college.
I'm an RA.

I put a rainbow flag on my door.
It gets torn down.
Damnit.

I buy another rainbow flag and put it on my door.
Someone writes all over it with black marker.
Damnit.

I buy another rainbow flag and put it on my door.
It gets torn down.
Damnit all to hell.

Pretty soon, the man behind the counter in the rainbow flag store
smiles when he sees me coming.

I think I'm keeping the rainbow flag store in business.

Flag Four disappeared.

"Fag" was written on Flag Five.

I think Flag Six just got nervous and skipped away.

Then Rainbow Flag Seven goes up.

I wait for it to get torn down.
Rainbow Flag Seven stays up.

I wait for the black marker.
Rainbow Flag Seven stays clean.

I wait for "fag".
Rainbow Flag Seven scoffs.

The rainbow flag store waits for me to keep them in business.
I never had to go back.

Somewhere in the waiting,
I realized I'm an activist.

I don't campaign.
I don't lobby.
I don't raise money.

I just have a flag.
Rainbow Flag Seven.
Still standing proud on my door.

*This submission is also available in poster format.
To purchase a poster please contact: The Collegiate EmPowerment Company
by calling toll free: 1-877-338-8246 or email: PosterInfo@Collegiate-EmPowerment.com.
Posters also be viewed and purchased online at: www.Collegiate-EmPowerment.com.
Thank you for your interest!

Where's My Community?
by Patricia Kevena Fili

The Struggle
To follow a Sacred Path
Is often Contradicted
By a Desire for Community.
Motivated to Play a Part
In Communicating that
Gender is a Continuum,
Compelled by the Spirit of Athena
To Fight
For Justice for Those
Who Transgress Gender Polarity,
Inspired by
Courageous Models and Martyred Angels
Who Risk Everything,
I Present an Imperfect Portrait.

All this is Tempered
By a Suicidal Brush
Which Counselled
That Self Care is not just Important,
But a Sacred Message
From Krishna Himself.

So I do what I do.
Searching for Venues
And Communities

That Renew
Where Necessity
Does not Require Me to Lead
Where I am as safe
As if the Protection of Amethyst
Safeguards Me Against all Ill
Honored, Accepted
As the woman I see in Reflection
From Within
And Without.

Then I Hear Honest
But Confused Musings
Declaring that Men Energy
Comes From
My Soul, My Body.
Me,
Who has Never Felt
One Day Like a Man.
Once Again,
The Safety I Felt
Flees From Me.
Once more,
Like a Circle
Not Understanding Alienation,
Like a Brother,
Not Understanding Difference,
Like a Daughter,
Not Wanting Contact

With a Cultural Pariah,
A Sanctuary I Longed For
Is Infected by an Ignorant Virus
So I ask,
Where do I go?
Where is my Community?
Perhaps with the Ghosts of Those
Who have Passed
Who Like Me,
Were Devoted
To Changing Consciousness
And Were Left
With that Pearl
As a Consolation
And the Loneliness
Of a Second Skin
That Always Reminds ▼

It's Not Easy Being Bi
by Ked Dixon

When it comes to relationships it sometimes seems more difficult to be an out bisexual than an out homosexual. As a bisexual, you are shunned, untrustworthy, greedy and capable of leaving your partner for literally the first person who crosses your path. Homosexuals are afraid that you will leave them for a member of the opposite sex, and heterosexuals are even more afraid that you will leave them for a member of your own sex.

The only exception is if you're a bisexual girl who is trying to break up with your boyfriend so you can date this cute girl you met at the dyke march and all he wants to do is watch you and this other girl get it on. He does not respect that your relationship with the girl is just as valid as your relationship with him. Or worse, he runs around telling everyone that he's turned you into a lesbian. Then you have to begin the painstaking process of teaching all of your friends about the mythical concept of bisexuality. At first, they will inevitably throw your idea to the four winds, claiming it's impossible to be mutually attracted to both sexes. You attain some sort of unicorn-like status things like you cannot exist. They can explain homosexuals with genes but where in the hell did you come from? Yes, life can be difficult when you're bi.

But it's not all hate and loneliness. The nicest thing about being bi is the very reason that makes a bisexual so suspicious. We can date anybody!! (With the exception of the homosexual members of the opposite sex and the heterosexual members of our own.) We are the go betweens of homosexuals and heterosexuals. We can fit in anywhere, and have fun doing it. I wouldn't trade my bisexuality for anything. ▼

The Usual
by Brian Coyle

The day began like every other, slinging hash and pouring coffee for a thankless commuter crowd. Grease wafted in the air, hung on the walls, and stuck in my pores. I've been doing this for too long! It was 7 a.m. and no sign of him. He, being my neighbor Tim across the hall in the apartments upstairs, was at the diner at 6:30 every day after his morning run. He's a cute kid, a creature of habit, always impeccably dressed with not a hair out of place. Even after his run. How does he do that?

"Good morning Liz," a voice called to me from behind as I was making a fresh pot of coffee with my back towards the counter.

The voice was familiar so I quickly replied, "You're late. It's 7:15". But as I turned around I almost didn't recognize the face.

It was Tim swimming in an extra large hooded sweatshirt, dirty jeans and a baseball cap. His baby blues were hidden behind a large, cheap pair of sunglasses.

"I'll have the usual," he said to me, his lips barely moving to mumble the words.

"Are you sure about that honey," I replied as I slid him a cup of coffee, "Because you don't look like the usual today."

"I'm fine, just getting a cold or something."

I noticed a bruise creeping out from behind his sunglasses. "I would have to guess the 'or something'," I said as I reached for the sunglasses and he winced as I removed them. "Oh dear God," was all I could think to say.

His right eye was almost swollen shut. His baby blues were

now black and blue and as my eyes drifted down in sympathy, I noticed more bruises and bite marks on his neck that the sweatshirt failed to hide.

"Maybe you better cancel that order, Liz. I'm not very hungry. It was a mistake to come here."

"Did he do this to you, honey?"

Tim flinched at my question. "No! Who? You don't know what you're talking about," he replied, panicked and agitated.

"Tim, it's okay. I'm not judging you, I just want to help." It was true. He was like one of my own kids now that they had grown up and left. I wanted to leap over that counter and hug him and tell him it would be all right, but my size 20 in motion would have injured him even more and drawn unwanted attention to his situation.

"You can't help," Tim spoke in a low voice, "Nobody can. You can't say a word to anyone, Liz. My life would be over!"

"Sweetie, your life could be over if you don't say anything. He could have killed you. Look at yourself!"

"Shhh, please Liz," his face begged. "I can't report this. I could lose my job and my parents and friends would disown me."

"Honey, you have got to call the police. If you don't, I will." Wouldn't any mother do the same? Wouldn't any person do the same if someone they cared about were in trouble?

"Oh, God," Tim sniffled and fought to hold back tears. "I can't do that to him. I can't ruin both of our lives. It was just an argument that got out of hand, really."

"Tim, did he....?"

His eyes betrayed him when he answered no and put his sunglasses back on.

"I'm here for you, anything you need Tim."

"Thanks… mom," he smiled at me and grabbed my hand gently. He did know. "Please don't say anything to anyone Liz, no matter what."

What could I do but grant the kid his only request?

"I'll see you tomorrow," he said as he pushed himself up from the counter and I prayed to God that I would. My heart broke as I watched him stagger and limp out of the diner. I hadn't seen him walk in and his injuries were obviously not limited to his face and neck.

When I got home that night from a double shift and my night class, several police cars were in front of the diner. Was there a robbery or an accident? Oh my God. Tim! I huffed and puffed my way as fast as I could up the stairs and down the dingy hallway. That scumbag finished him off. I should have done something. I have to tell them. I don't care what Tim wanted.

There were two officers in the hall outside Tim's open door. I managed to yell out, "What happened?" between breaths. I think my heart actually stopped beating. I thought I had been through it all in my years on this earth, but I don't think I have the strength to walk through that door and identify his body.

The police said nothing and scooted me into Tim's apartment. I found myself able to breath again when I saw him sitting on the couch, giving his statement to the police.

"You were right Liz, about everything," Tim said as he lifted his head from his hands. "He came back and tried to hurt me again. I told him it was over and I called the police. I know I don't deserve this. This is Janice," he said motioning towards a woman seated in a nearby chair, "and she runs a program that's going to help remind me of that."

A smile and a faint glimpse of the old Tim flashed across his face.

"I am very pleased to meet you Janice," I said as I choked back my tears of pride. I think of myself as a pretty gutsy person, but this kid's got more courage than anyone I've ever known. "You take good care of my boy." ▼

Hidden Path
by Setheriane Adams

Day of Silence.
Showing the silence brought about by the deaths of others.
Showing that we care.
Making a statement.
A GSA falling apart.
People forgetting.
Leaving.
Not caring at all.
Started out wonderfully.
Then all the controversy wore off.
Without a fight the passion wasn't there.

Nothing to do to bring us together.
Except the Day of Silence.
Three days to put it together.
Announcements.
Flyers.
Handouts.
Black arm bands to symbolize your involvement.
Hoping it will fly and people help out.

Three days ticks away.
It's the big day.
Walking through the halls.
Looking at the others wearing the arm band.

A GSA with five members.
Multiply that by infinity.
That's how you find the number of supporters we saw.
Everywhere you turned another black arm band.

We run out of arm bands.
Kids staple and tape black paper around their arms.
The end of the day comes.
We're proud.
We finally touched them.
We finally made an impact.
A struggling GSA found it's path. ▼

*This submission is also available in poster format.
To purchase a poster please contact: The Collegiate EmPowerment Company
by calling toll free: 1-877-338-8246 or email: PosterInfo@Collegiate-EmPowerment.com.
Posters also be viewed and purchased online at: www.Collegiate-EmPowerment.com.
Thank you for your interest!

I've Passed The Bar!
by Dana DeAndrea Turner, J.D.

All my life I have been engaged in one endeavor - passing the New York bar examination. After six tries, $1,500 in fees to the State of New York and way more than $5,000 in bar review course tuition fees, books and materials, I, Dana DeAndra Turner, have been certified for admission to the New York State Bar by virtue of having PASSED the administration of the New York State Bar examination! I am having difficulty believing it, but, my long awaited dream is actually coming true.

No matter what anyone tells you, it takes more than a dream, determination and a little talent to enter the echelon of licensed professionals in America. Especially if you are gay, or African-American, not to mention if you are a transsexual - and I am all three. I've realized that I am not competing for jobs that many think ought not go to someone of my social strata, sexual orientation or gender classification. When you know there are people 'out there' who do not wish you success the struggle becomes even more difficult - but the victory of succeeding in spite of them is heady and empowering.

My own mother who has been a Jehovah's Witness for the past 40 years was one of the people hovering in and out of my life who did not approve of my 'big dreams' and unbridled pursuit of them. When you fail or mess-up you think, "maybe 'they' are right." But they're not. Your dream is your own and no one can douse it. I've think I'm beginning to learn that.

I didn't enter law school until I was 31 and I attended five different colleges - community, junior, technical and otherwise - before I finally got a BA from Portland State University. I graduated from law school with a Juris Doctor degree nine years ago but I was too paralyzed with fear and doubt to take the next necessary steps towards my personal empowerment - realizing my dreams. My dreams changed and grew and developed and solidified, but I seemed to always be in pursuit of them. Sometimes I had seemingly conflicting dreams, but I kept them.

I dreamed of living in New York City, first as a fashion designer, then as a dancer, then most recently as an attorney. My legal career is just an adjunct to my other dreams, the sum of which make up who I am, and who I want to be. And I am still dreaming.

In 1993, I put the dream of a career in law on hold to answer another call. A lifelong desire to be who I really was. Simple for most folks, but not for me. Changing my sex has meant a lot of sacrifices, financial and otherwise, but it too has been worth it. And now with the realization of another side of myself I cannot help but to think about the many other people like me, who had the same dreams, but never had the chance to see them come true. And, I think about the few people I know like me that have been able to achieve some of our similar dream, but we are not many.

Due to the nature of transsexual identity, we can never really know who or when the first transsexual lawyer or lawyers practicing in New York were, or have been. However, I do know that I am not the first. I am just the most recent in a long and enduring line of legal practioners who chose New York as the place where they could live their true lives. Some of them are known to us, and some of them may never be known.

There was the 15th English governor of the colonies of New York and New Jersey, Viscount Cornbury Lord Edward Hyde;

whom, after his appointment in 1702, earned public approbation for his penchant for dressing up like his first cousin, Queen Anne, and trolling Broad Street ... there's even an 18th-century portrait of him dressed in all his queenly regalia in the collections of the New York Historical Society. He/she was deposed for land graft in 1708.

Then there was the Tammany Hall wheeler-dealer politician and New York City bail bondsman - (a form of 'legal' practice if ever there was one) - named Murray Hall; who married twice, drank heavily and got locked up once for giving a cop a black eye. Only upon his death in 1901 at age 70 was it discovered that he was a transman.

And in the 1980s there was New York's first 'out' African-American male-to-female transsexual attorney, Ariel Makela, who worked at the NYC Human Rights Commission. I saw Ariel on an Geraldo Rivera show in about 1988. She was beautiful, and I was inspired. I was on hiatus [can you say 'dropout?'] from my second year of law school at Georgetown and seriously reconsidering the whole idea of law - period, as I still do. When I saw Ariel Makela I realized my dreams really could come true: To live and work in New York City as an attorney in the gender I was born to live in. And today, that dream has become my reality. ▼

A Tale of Hope
by Smokie Joe Egaltor

I will tell you the tale of how hope began.
Wandering through life empty and alone.
It began with "Hello".

I will tell you the tale of how hope began.
Helpless, hopeless and sure there was no way out.
It began with "I can help you".

I will tell you the tale of how hope began.
Stuffed with doubt, fear and confusion.
It began with "It's okay, let it out".

I will tell you the tale of how hope began.
Exploding at the edges, everything flying out.
It began with "I hear you".

I will tell you the tale of how hope began.
Sadness, guilt, shame, worthless and in pain, oh so much pain.
It began with "I'm here for you".

And you said Hello,
And you are helping,
And I am letting it out,
And I am being heard,
And you ARE here for me.
I will tell you the tale of how hope began.
With time and trust, opening up and running away.
It began with ME. ▼

Power Reframe
by Ted Burnes

She's got a Bush…Cheney sticker on her SUV,
She's beautiful, she bright-eyed, she's as happy as can be,
She did what she wanted, she loved it all plus more;
And now it's a challenge to walk out her front door.
He told her it was fun and that she should just "enjoy",
She screamed "no" eighty times, but he treated her like a toy.
He raped her, and now she's a survivor – bye-bye goes the dream,
And the scars from that episode are worse than they might seem.

So, he went to this little party, thought he'd meet a hot new guy.
He had a couple of drinks and realized his game was pretty fly.
Another man walked up and said,
"You're cute, you're place or mine?"
Our guy smiled, saying, "I'm not looking for just sex…
no thanks, I'm just fine."
And then the room started to spin,
and the voices faded in and out,
The roofie had taken its effect and our boy's safety is in doubt.
It was over in three minutes, and bodily fluids were exchanged.
Our boy didn't remember a thing
And his life was rearranged.

These two peeps got RAPED, my people,
And it happens every hour.
Because whether or not you want to admit it,
It's a fucked up exchange of power.

Perhaps we need to look at these exchanges,
With some phat revolution eyes.
And let's not forgot that victims of assault also happen to be guys.
So, if you see someone in a weird situation,
I empower you – take a stand!
Walk right up to that sketchball, and tell him
"MOVE YOUR GODDAMN HAND!"
Walk right up to that lady and say,
"I think my friend said 'no'".
And if she gives you any shit, say "Leave, 'cause I said so."
let's start a fight back on assault, and let's start it from right here.
men may be from Mars and women from Venus,
but their communication can be clear!
no one deserves to be assaulted,
so no longer shall we cower.
let's help those out there who live in fear
and redistribute the power ▼

Something Better To Do
by Dan Woog

It came, as these things so often do, anonymously. It came to the OutSpoken youth group with a local postmark, but bore no return address. These things never do.

For over eight years I have been a co-facilitator of Out- Spoken -- a support group for gay, lesbian, bisexual, transgender and questioning youth. In those eight years, over 800 young people from Fairfield County, Connecticut -- and beyond -- have walked through our doors. We have welcomed teenagers as young as 13, boys and girls who were as certain of their sexuality as they were of their name; their parents brought them, and thanked us for what we do. We have welcomed 20-somethings, less sure of who they are; chronologically they are young adults, but emotionally they still struggle. Each young person has an incredible story to tell, about the life journey that has brought him or her to OutSpoken. I am in awe of their maturity, courage and sense of self.

Which is why I was so stunned when I opened that anonymous letter last month. It contained a copy of "Update," the newsletter of Exodus North America. The group's tagline reads: "Freedom from Homosexuality Through the Power of Jesus Christ." The lead story featured a photo of a somber-looking woman, Jill Postell. She authored the tale, headlined "No More Hiding." It began: "I was a Bible college student but also a practicing lesbian. My double life made me feel like a hypocrite and a failure. How can I find help?" God, she said two pages later, delivered her from the horror of homosexuality.

As I read, I thought about the discussions we've had at OutSpoken over the past eight years. They have ranged far and wide, from coming out to friends and family, to meeting other gay young people, to the importance of safer sex. Our discussions have been intense, intriguing, uproarious, tearful, challenging, and often joyous. Almost always, they have centered around the deep need we -- every human being -- has for being accepted and loved for who we are. Some of the youngsters (and facilitators) at OutSpoken are deeply religious; others have not been inside a church or synagogue in years. Virtually all, however, are spiritually strong, in whatever way works best for us.

I thought about all that as I read the Exodus newsletter, and the religious tracts that accompanied the anonymous mailing. "Where are you going to spend eternity?" one asked. Another demanded that I acknowledge myself as a sinner. A third commanded me to check one of two boxes:"I choose to trust Jesus as my saviour," or "I choose to reject Jesus and keep my way."

I thought how truthful and honest the young people at OutSpoken are, and how proud I am that they live their lives with integrity. I thought how cowardly it is to send an anonymous mailing, and how hateful and spiteful the "God-fearing" man or woman must be who sent this to our group. I thought about all this, and then I did the only thing I could: I threw it in the trash. I could not waste another moment worrying about such close-minded people. I had something far more important thing to do: I had an OutSpoken meeting to help run. ▼

I'm Her Son Again
by Myke Silvestri

My senior year of high school, I was accepted to the University of Connecticut. My mom had worked at UConn for a good portion of my life, so my family has some pretty good ties there.

The moment my parents drove away, I was out looking for other people like me. I found UConn's Rainbow Center, a cultural center for the glbt community, and I found AQUA, the Allies and Queers Undergraduate Association.

I attended AQUA's first meeting, and saw that they needed alot of help. I ran for office as secretary, and won. My name was printed on a few lists here and there, which kind of worried me. I wasn't out to my parents, and my mom was in a fairly important position on campus, and knew a lot of people.

I did this for a semester, getting involved in a lot of Queer issues and events on campus, networking with important offices, and moved home for winter break. Near the end of break, my mom was joking around with me as she often did, and asked the question. "Are you gay?"

It wasn't the first time she'd asked me this. But up until college, I'd considered myself bisexual, and was able to justify saying "no." But it wasn't high school anymore. So I asked her what she would say if I said "yes" one of these times. She responded saying that she would be a little disappointed that she wouldn't have grandchildren from me, but that she'd be okay. So I said it. "Cause I am."

She made me tell my father. My full-blooded, born-and-raised Sicilian father. He sat silent for a while. And asked "How can you know?" and told me "No you're not." Then he sent me to my room.

I woke up in the morning to a very loud angry pounding on my door. My mother was standing there, in tears. She started yelling at me. She told me how I was being inconsiderate, and doing this for attention. I was embarrassing her, and she couldn't even drive to work because UConn reminded her of me. She wished I'd moved further away instead of staying so close. My father wasn't talking to her about it, so I was ruining my family. Our family already had alcoholics, drug addicts, mental cases, and now "we've got a faggot." Then she informed me that when I moved back for the spring semester, I wasn't welcome back in my home. She couldn't bear to look at my face.

I left for the semester expecting to return once when nobody was home to move boxes they were letting me keep in my room. I had been offered a deal, where I could keep their financial aid, and move back in the summer... but only if I gave up being gay on campus. No AQUA, no boyfriends... nothing. I accepted, but knew I had no intentions of keeping it.

Right before Spring Break, I happened to talk to my mom. This was one of the first few times since I moved back. She had found out that not only had I broken my agreement, but I had run for co-chair of AQUA, and was one of the more visible Queers on campus. We got into a big argument, and she told me she didn't care where I was going for spring break, she didn't have to.

Over spring break, I got into a bad situation with an older man because I needed a place to stay for two days and a ride to the bus station. I visited a high school friend a few states away at her college, and came back to stay with a UConn friend for the remainder of break. While with the last friend, I was driving a car not my own, and we hit a big-rig truck (his fault, for the record) and were lucky to escape the wreck with our lives. I didn't call my parents.

They found out through my insurance company, and called me, very upset. This was the turning point. After a conversation I was welcome to come home, with no conditions, though "I knew how they felt" about things.

I never talked about being gay unless they brought it up first. It was like being in the closet, except I didn't have to worry as much about them finding out. I moved back to school, and things were the same for a while. Slowly, my mom began to start accepting things, and trying to cope with humor. She made a joke here or there... some of which I found a little offensive... but I educated her where I could, and let a lot slide because of circumstances.

The spring semester a full year after I told them held a huge, and encouraging surprise. My sister and mother were at an incoming freshman event on campus, and I walked down to meet them for lunch. When my mom walked out of an activities fair they were at, she was wearing a rainbow striped "Celebrate Diversity" pin that she'd picked up at the Rainbow Center table. My mother, the woman who had kicked me out of the house for ruining my family, was wearing a GAY PIN. I was speechless.

Since then, I've started to build back the close relationship I'd had with my mother up until the part of high school that started dealing with sexuality. I've included AQUA and Rainbow Center events I've attended and spoke at in my anecdotes about UConn... and I think she might even be becoming proud of the way I've decided to live my life. She's realizing that I still have the same morals she raised me with, I'm still kind and compassionate to others, and I definitely still stand up for what I believe in, and am not going to let anyone think they're better than me just because they happened to be born/raised into a more acceptable orientation. She's realizing I still have the same morals with which she raised me. I'm still kind and compassionate to others. I'm still standing up for what I believe in. I'm her son again! ▼

An Ally's Promise
by Anthony J. D'Angelo

I believe...
I believe success is the freedom to be yourself.
I believe nobody is wrong they are only different.
I believe your circumstances don't define you,
rather they reveal you.
I believe without a sense of caring,
there can be no sense of community.
I believe our minds are like parachutes.
They only work if they are open.
I believe we only live life once,
but if we live it right, one time is all we'll need.
I believe we must first get along with ourselves
before we can get along with others.

I will...
I will seek to understand you.
I will label bottles, not people.
I will grow antennas not horns.
I will see the diversity of our commonality.
I will see the commonality of our diversity.
I will get to know who you are rather than what you are.
I will transcend political correctness
and strive for human righteousness.

I challenge you...
I challenge you to honor who you are.
I challenge you to enjoy your life rather than endure it.
I challenge you to create the status quo rather than accept it.
I challenge you to live in your imagination
more than your memory.
I challenge you to live your life as a revolution
and not just a process of evolution.
I challenge you to ignore other people's ignorance
so that you may discover your own wisdom.

I promise you...
I promise to do my part.
I promise to stand beside you.
I promise to interrupt the world
when its thinking becomes ignorant.
I promise to believe in you,
even when you have lost faith in yourself.

I am here for you. ▼

The Inspiration Book Series

Lavender Graduation:
OUR Ceremony On Campus
by Ronni Sanlo

It was like magic. Who would have thought that such an event would take place here as an official UCLA commencement?

Such a simple concept: to honor lesbian, gay, bisexual, and transgender (LGBT) students for the gifts they brought to campus and for the achievements they had as a result of having been in college. So simple a way to tell students they matter…

This was so fantastic! I got chills! I'll be there when I graduate.

Until 1995, there were no ceremonies to honor our LGBT students. There were ceremonies for students of various ethnicities and for other non-academic groups like ROTC, but nothing for our students, those who tend to feel to most disenfranchised from their colleges and universities.

My parents finally understand why I'm out. Thank You!

Unfortunately, there are no data that describe positive celebratory events in the lives of LGBT college students.

It was so inspiring and affirming. I loved it!
Thanks for a wonderful memory.

In fact, scant literature describes celebratory experiences in the general LGBT culture(s). LGBT students usually experience the culture of their ethnic, racial, religious, or national backgrounds, but rarely experience a university-supported event directly associated with their lives as LGBT people and LGBT students.

I finally feel like I belong at UCLA, ironically, just as I am leaving.

Celebration events provide significant impact on the lives of students. Lavender Graduation is an event to which LGBT students look forward, where they not only share their hopes and dreams with one another, but are officially recognized by the institution for their leadership and their successes and achievements.

I felt very honored to be part of Lavender Graduation.

When I was director of the LGBT campus resource center at the University of Michigan years ago, I realized that LGBT students deserved to be recognized not only for their achievements but for surviving their college years. As the planning of commencement activities for 1995 took place, I saw an opportunity to include LGBT students in the celebratory process. Many ethnic groups were hosting their own ceremonies, so why not us? I often heard from LGBT students that they didn't feel connected to the university nor their departments or even to their ethnic groups so they choose not to participate in commencement ceremonies. LGBT students said their journeys through college as out people had been painful enough. They wanted to leave quickly and quietly.

This was so encouraging. I can't wait until my own Lavender Graduation in two years.

I am a lesbian Jewish mother. I love celebrations, so I created Lavender Graduation, an event that intersects both my religion and my sexual orientation. Lavender is important to LGBT history. It combines the pink triangle that gay men were forced to wear and the black triangle designating lesbians as political prisoners in Nazi Germany. LGBT activists took these symbols of hatred, combined them, and created a symbol and color of pride and community.

It felt great being here. I felt like my work was worth it, that I finally counted here.

When I moved to UCLA in 1997 as the director of the LGBT Campus Resource Center, I brought Lavender Graduation with me. With national keynote speakers, entertainment, leadership awards, and rainbow tassels, the event became an instant and popular success.

I'm here because I wanted to support and congratulate my friends. I know they'll be here for my Lavender Graduation.

Over the years since the first ceremony in 1995, members of the National Consortium of Directors of Resources in Higher Education (www.lgbtcampus.org) have begun hosting Lavender Graduations celebrations at their institutions as well.

I went to Lavender Graduation and really got inspired to start doing something active in the community.

My vision is that Lavender Graduation will be an annual celebration at every college and university in the country and that the lives of our LGBT students will be fully honored. Since LGBT students are of every race, ability, nationality, gender, ethnicity, and socioeconomic levels, Lavender Graduation provides a unique opportunity to present a truly multicultural event while acknowledging students who spent most of their college years succumbing to invisibility on their campuses.

Totally inspirational.

Lavender Graduation makes a strong institutional statement to LGBT college students: It tells them that they matter.

I just want to thank you for an amazing Lavender ceremony. It was fun and personal, an experience that I'll never forget. ▼

Lavender Graduation photo by Carol Petersen

Permissions & Trademarks

We would like to thank the following contributing authors for their permission to reprint their submissions.

The Lambda 10 Project

Gay, Lesbian, Bisexual Fraternity & Sorority Issues

What is the Lambda 10 Project?

The Lambda 10 Project - National Clearinghouse for Gay, Lesbian, Bisexual Fraternity & Sorority Issues works to heighten the visibility of gay, lesbian, and bisexual members of the college fraternity Lambda 10 Project was founded in the Fall of 1995 and serves as a clearinghouse for educational resources and educational materials related to sexual orientation and the fraternity/sorority experience. The Lambda 10 Project created the first educational resources solely dedicated to this topic titled "Out on Fraternity Row: Personal Accounts of Being Gay in a College Fraternity" released by Alyson Publications, Inc in 1998 and "Secret Sisters: Stories of Being Lesbian & Bisexual in a College Sorority" released by Alyson Publications, Inc. in April 2001.

Online features, the marketplace, chats, bulletin board, anti-homophobia training manuals, educational exercises & handouts, guest speakers, and the premiere Who's Out listing are among the various products and services provided by the Lambda 10 Project at www.lambda10.org.

For more information, call 704-277-6710 or email info@lambda10.org or check us out online at www.lambda10.org

Campus PrideNet
National Online Network for LGBT Student Leaders

What is Campus PrideNet?

Campus PrideNet is a national online network and resource clearinghouse committed to student leaders and campus organizations who work to create a safer campus environment free of homophobia, biphobia, transphobia, heterosexism and genderism at colleges and universities.

Our Vision

Campus PrideNet envisions a safer campus environment free of homophobia, biphobia, transphobia, heterosexism and genderism at colleges and universities and works to develop student leaders, campus networks, and organizations to create such positive change.

Our Values

- Utilizing the diverse talents of student leaders.
- Giving students a voice and action in leadership.
- Empowering student leaders for positive change in society.
- Building stronger glbtq communities on college campuses.
- Celebrating and recognizing diversity.

**For more information, call 704-277-6710
or email info@campuspride.net
or check us out online at www.campuspride.net**

An Overview Of
The Collegiate EmPowerment Company, Inc.

"Helping You Take Higher Education Deeper™"

The Collegiate EmPowerment Company is a nationally recognized educational firm dedicated to empowering college students & student affairs professionals with the most interactive, inspiring and informative empowerment seminars & products.

We are the only organization in the world solely dedicated to serving college students & student affairs professionals. Since 1995 we have served over 1 million students & clients from over 1000 colleges across North America, The United Kingdom & Australia.

In addition to the Inspiration Book Series™ We serve college students & student affairs professional like you with the following tools & resources:

"Young Adults EmPowering Young Adults"

EmPower X! is the instructional team of The Collegiate EmPowerment Company. EmPower X! is an elite kick ass team of young & professional adults, all under the age of 30, who facilitate the What College Forgets To Teach You® Seminars. Each member of EmPower X! is a Certified Collegiate EmPowerment Coach™, who has been hand selected & personally trained by Anthony J. D'Angelo.

What College Forgets to Teach You® The cornerstone of the Collegiate EmPowerment Company is its What College Forgets To Teach You® Seminar Series. A curriculum series of over 30 comprehensive & integrated seminars, created by Anthony D'Angelo, exclusively designed to address the challenges typical of most college students & university graduates. The series consists of four different levels of seminars, each containing distinct concepts, tools, strategies and systems. Each seminar reinforces the others and deepens a student's understanding of his or her own vision & purpose in life.

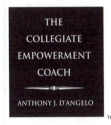

THE COLLEGIATE EMPOWERMENT COACH

ANTHONY J. D'ANGELO

The man who is Helping You Take Higher Education Deeper™ & the Founder of The Collegiate EmPowerment Company, Anthony J. D'Angelo. He has been hailed by CNNfn as, "The Personal Development Guru Of His Generation" and SPIN Magazine has compared D'Angelo with the likes of world renowned peak performance expert, Anthony Robbins.

Today Anthony serves as the Chief Visionary Officer of The CEC & is the creator of The Inspiration Book Series and the architect of EmPower X!. He is also the #1 Contributing Author and Editor of The New York Times Bestseller, Chicken Soup For The College Soul. His current projects include the expansion of The Inspiration Book Series™ & The What College Forgets To Teach You® Multimedia Transformation System. In addition, Anthony provides one-to-one coaching services to highly motivated & committed professionals and student leaders.

FOR MORE INFORMATION CALL: 1.877.338.8246
OR VISIT US ONLINE AT WWW.COLLEGIATE-EMPOWERMENT.COM

WOULD YOU LIKE TO SEE YOUR STORY IN INSPIRATION FOR LGBT STUDENTS & THEIR ALLIES™ VOLUME II?

All of the stories that you have read in this book were submitted by people like you. We would love to have you contribute a story, poem, quote or cartoon to:

Inspiration for LGBT Students & Their Allies™ Volume II

Even though we are planning to launch several other Inspiration Books over the next few years, (see inside front cover for details) we are always looking for more LGBT Stories to create Volume II.

Feel free to send us stories you write yourself. It also could be a favorite poem, quotation, cartoon or story you have seen that speaks to your experience. Just make sure to send as much information about you and the source of your submission.

Please fax or email your submissions to:
The Collegiate EmPowerment Company, Inc.
Fax: 610-252-6946
Email: Inspiration@Collegiate-EmPowerment.com

If your submission is accepted & approved your message will touch the lives of thousands of students across the country!
(Of course you'll get a free book too!)